Mind Maps

Biology for Kids

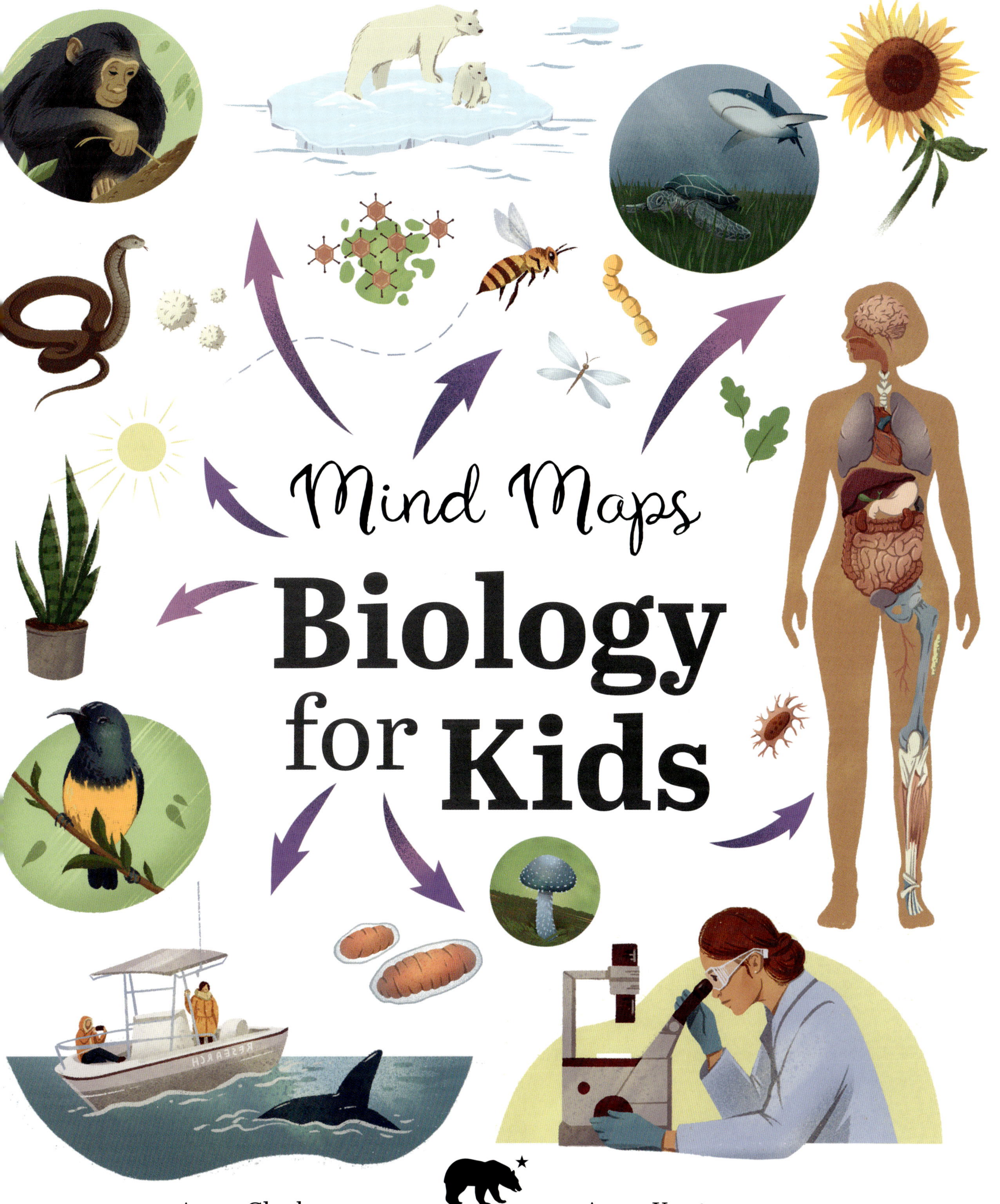

Anna Claybourne

ARCTURUS

Anna Kuptsova

This edition published in 2025 by
Arcturus Publishing Limited
26/27 Bickels Yard, 151–153 Bermondsey Street, London SW1 3HA

ISBN: 978-1-3988-4469-8
CH011050US

Author: Anna Claybourne
Illustrator: Anna Kuptsova
Consultant: Tom Jackson
Designer: Sally Bond
Design Manager: Rosie Bellwood-Moyler
Editors: Lydia Halliday and Coffee Cup Creative
Editorial Manager: Joe Harris

Supplier 29, Date 0425, Print run 00006658

Printed in China

How this book works

In science, everything is connected!

Biology is the science of life and living things, including animals, plants, tiny bacteria, and the human body. Just as in other areas of science, all living things and life-science topics are connected.

For example, imagine you're studying cells, the tiny building blocks that living things are made of. This topic links to many others in biology, such as ...

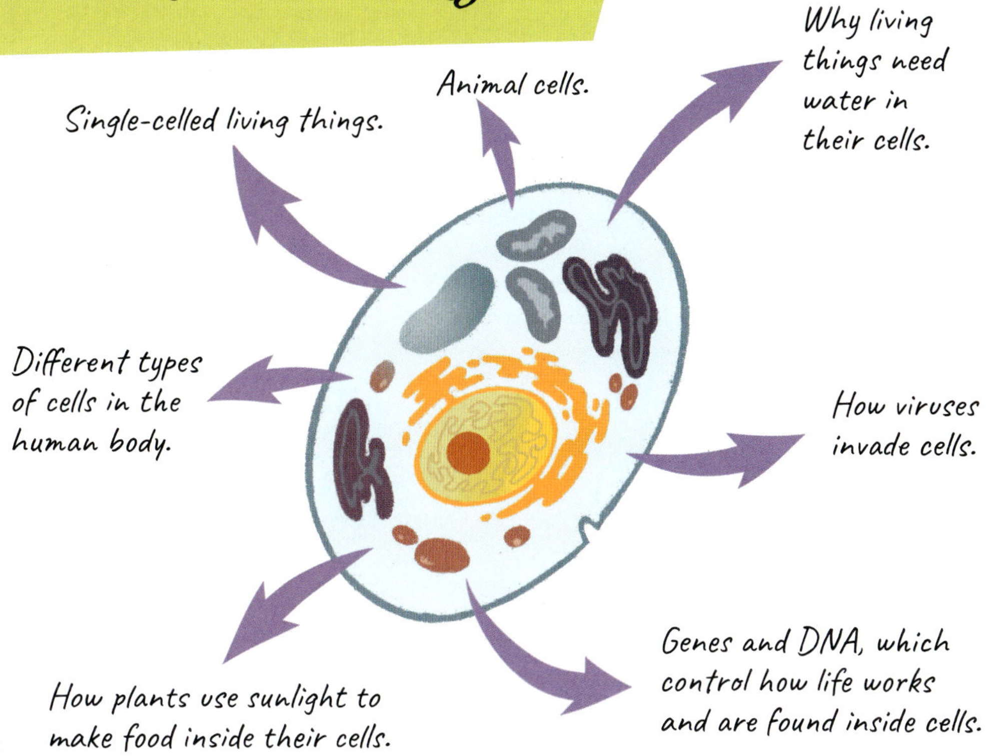

Make the link ...

This book links topics together in a big mind map, so you can see how everything is connected. Whenever there's a connection to a related topic, you'll find a link, like this.

You can read the different sections and topics in any order, or just choose a topic you're interested in using the content diagram on the next page. Then follow the links to find out more, or jump to a different page and explore!

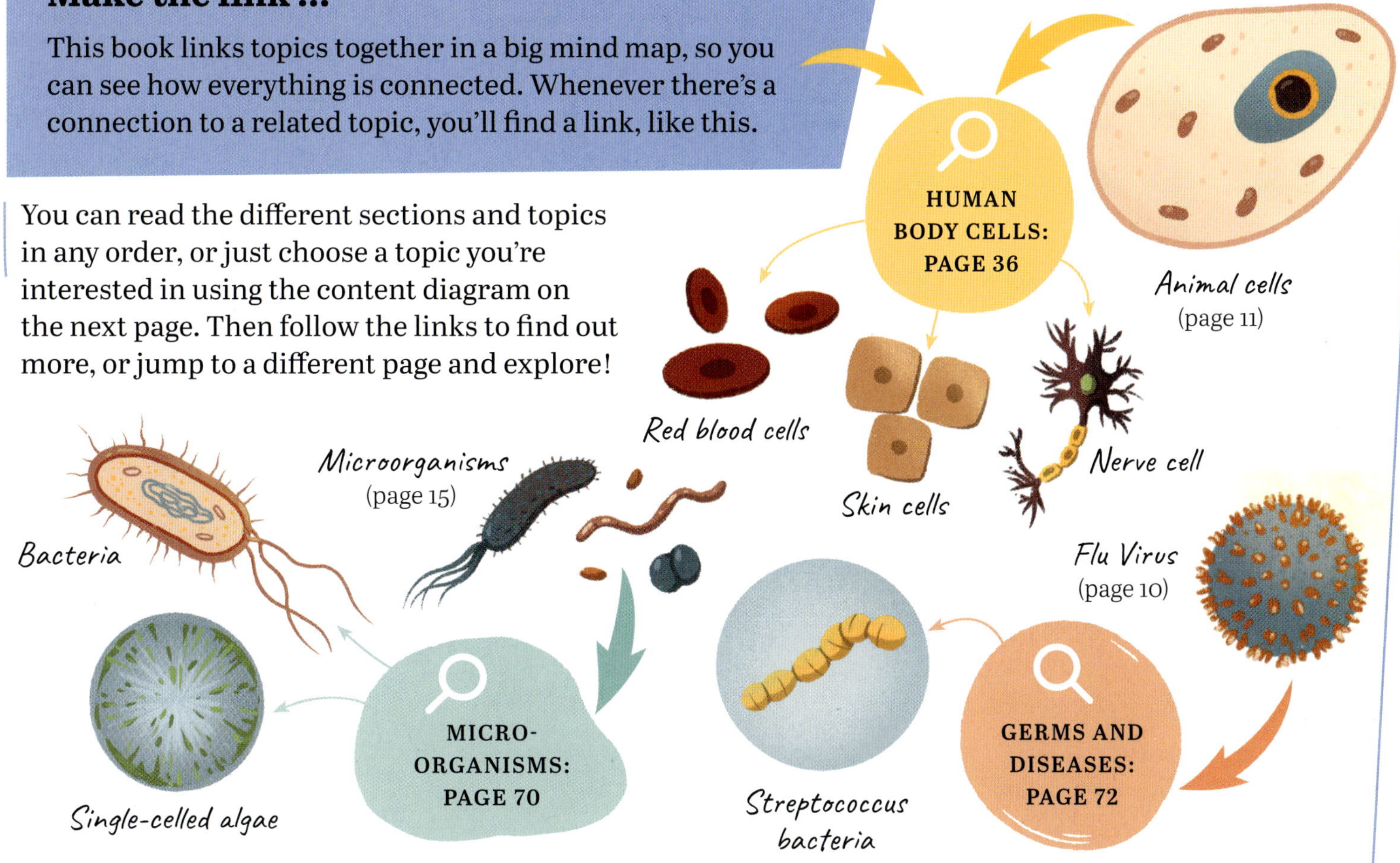

What's in the book?

Here are all the biology topics you'll find in this handy book.

Use the page numbers to find the topic you want, or just dip in at random!

What is life?

Animals

The human body

Plants and fungi

Microbiology

Look out for the links to different topics on each page, like this:

FUNGI:
PAGE 64

Living planet

What is life?

Living things are all around us, and we humans are living things too. When you see a dog, a bee, or a plant growing, you know they're alive. But what exactly is a living thing, and what do they all have in common?

Living things come in a variety of different types, or species—from tiny creepy crawlies and invisible germs, to towering trees and whales that travel the world. But they all have something in common—seven things, in fact!

Something is only alive if it does all of these things!

- Moving
- Feeding
- Respiring
- Growing
- Excreting
- Sensing
- Reproducing

Giant pandas are a living species. They have all seven signs of life.

Clouds aren't alive! Although they do move and sometimes grow, they don't have any of the other signs of life.

Types of living things

Living things fall into several main types, including ...

CLASSIFICATION: PAGE 14

MORE

Morpho butterfly

Sunflower

Fly agaric toadstool

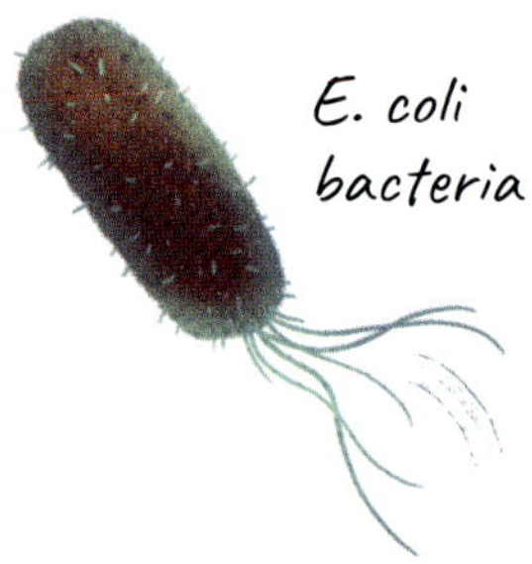

E. coli bacteria

Animals

Such as dogs, cats, worms, pandas, fish, snakes, insects, and humans.

Plants

Such as daisies, sunflowers, trees, bushes, ferns, grass, and moss.

Fungi

Such as mushrooms and toadstools, mold and yeast.

Microorganisms

Single-celled organisms such as bacteria, amoebas, and other tiny lifeforms.

ANIMALS: PAGE 20

PLANTS: PAGE 52

FUNGI: PAGE 64

MICROBIOLOGY: PAGE 68

Moving

All living things can move, though some move more than others ...

PLANTS: PAGE 52

ANIMALS: PAGE 20

Feeding

Living things take in food, whether by eating, or by using other ingredients to make food, like plants do.

PHOTOSYNTHESIS: PAGE 54

Respiring

Respiring means turning food into energy, which all living things need.

Growing

Living things use the food they take in to grow and make new cells or body parts.

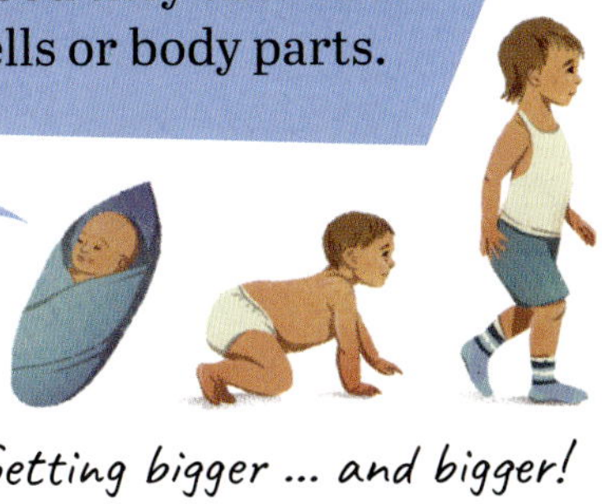

STAGES OF LIFE: PAGE 48

Excreting

Taking in food and turning it into energy makes waste, such as urine (pee). Living things "excrete" or empty out this waste—like when you go to the toilet.

DIGESTIVE SYSTEM: PAGE 40

Sensing

Living things can sense their surroundings—like when a spider feels vibrations in its web, or a plant senses water.

INVERTEBRATES: PAGE 24

Reproducing

Finally, all species of living things can reproduce, or make copies of themselves.

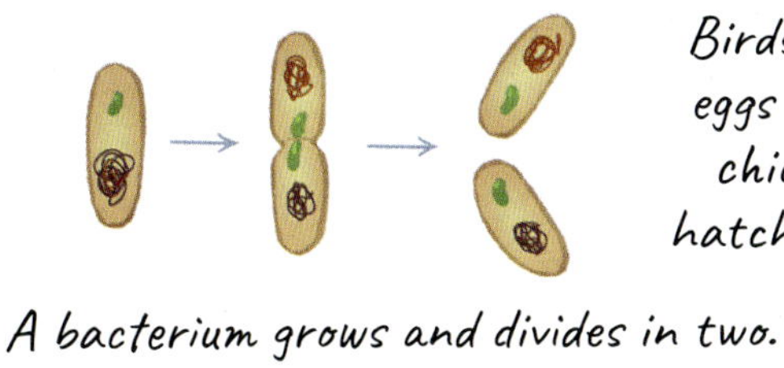

PLANTS: PAGE 52

BIRDS: PAGE 23

MICROBIOLOGY: PAGE 68

Biology and biologists

"Bio" means life, so "biology" means the study of life and living things. People who study this science are known as biologists. There are thousands and thousands of them, studying every kind of living thing you can imagine!

Biologists study living things by observing or watching them, measuring and counting them, and doing experiments, such as testing which temperatures make bacteria grow fastest.

This biologist is using a microscope to look at a sample of soil to see what's living in it. She's spotted a tardigrade, a tiny animal less than 1 mm (.04 in) long.

Tardigrade

Biologists get to work in a variety of different places, including science labs, classrooms, and out and about in forests, deserts, under the sea, or anywhere else living things are found ...

Groups or "colonies" of bacteria growing in a glass container called a petri dish.

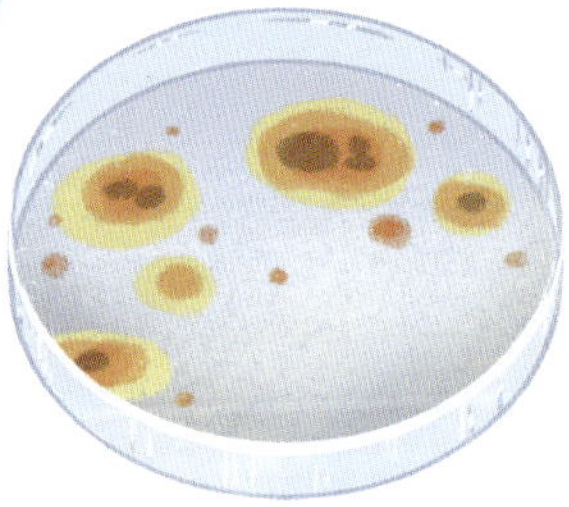

Biologists use lots of equipment, such as microscopes, petri dishes, insect-catching nets, and sound recorders.

MICROBIOLOGY: PAGE 68

MORE

Areas of biology

Biology is a big subject, so many biologists focus on a particular area, or type of biology. These include ...

Botany—the study of plants.
Zoology—the study of animals.
Mycology—the study of fungi.
Microbiology—the study of microorganisms.
Marine biology—the study of sea life.
Ecology—ecosystems and habitats.
Taxonomy—the classification of living things.
Genetics—the study of genes and DNA.
Cytology—the study of cells.

HABITATS: PAGE 76

CLASSIFICATION: PAGE 14

CELLS: PAGE 10

In the field

"The field" is what scientists call the real world, where they study things in their natural surroundings. Wildlife can be shy, hard to find, or even dangerous, so biologists have to be careful. They often spend a long time searching for the living things they want to study.

This biologist is counting tiger tracks and poop to calculate how many endangered tigers are living in a wildlife reserve.

ENDANGERED SPECIES: PAGE 86

CONSERVATION: PAGE 88

In the lab

In a biology lab, biologists can use science equipment to study living things more closely, and do experiments to find things out.

How do the light-sensing cells in our eyes detect different hues?

HUMAN CELLS: PAGE 36

Do plants grow faster if you play music to them?

Can a squirrel solve a puzzle to get a hazelnut reward?

ANIMAL BRAINS: PAGE 30

Universities and museums

As well as studying, some biologists work as teachers in universities, teaching biology to students. Others work in museums, making displays for visitors, or looking after collections of biology samples, such as seashells or bones.

INVERTEBRATES: PAGE 24

Seashell collection

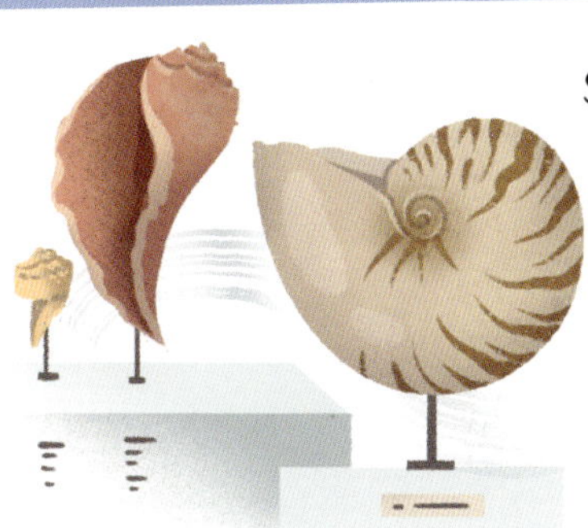

Seashell display

Teaching students

Cells

When you look at a leaf, an insect, or your own arm, you're looking at cells! They're the tiny units that living things are built from. There are billions of cells in a human, a tree, or an elephant, but there are also many organisms that have just one cell each.

A typical cell has these parts:

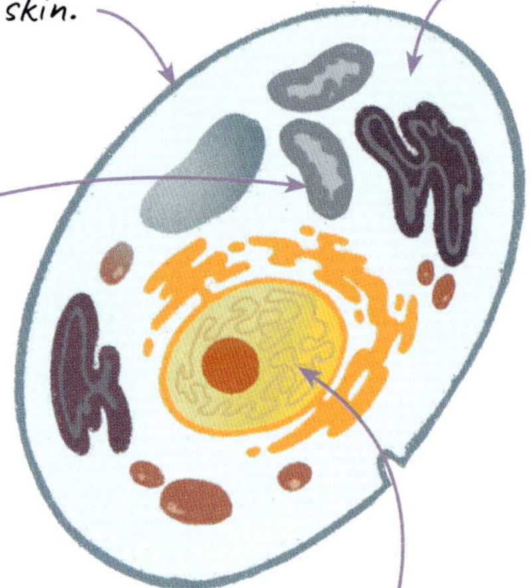

Mitochondria are organelles (meaning mini-organs). Organelles do different jobs inside the cell and there are many types.

There are several types of cells, including:

- Animal cells
- Plant cells
- Tiny single-celled living things, such as bacteria

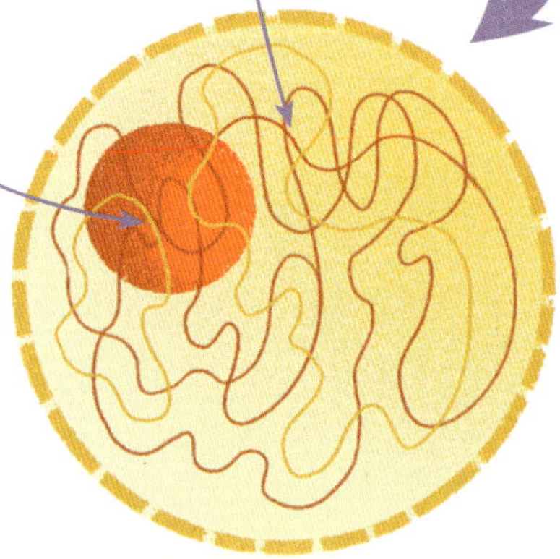

GENES AND DNA: PAGE 12

Cell HQ

Many cells have a nucleus. It contains DNA, a string-shaped chemical that can store instructions, known as genes.

The cell follows the instructions in the genes in order to do different jobs.

MORE

Viruses

Viruses are much smaller than cells, and are not fully alive. They invade and hijack cells to make them produce more viruses, but they can't reproduce on their own.

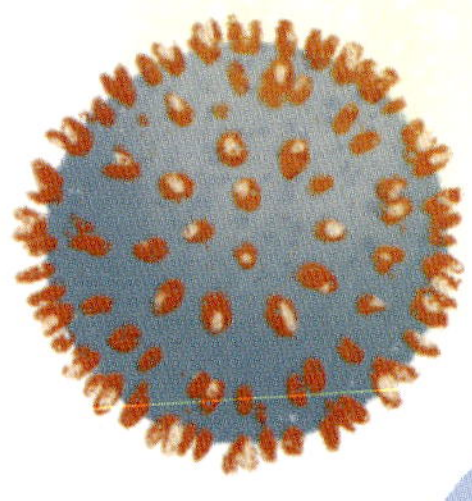

GERMS AND DISEASES: PAGE 50

Animal cells

An animal cell usually has an uneven shape and a flexible cell membrane.

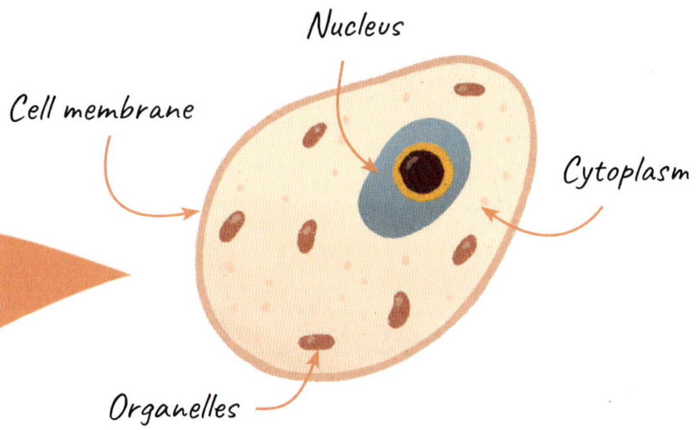

Types of cells

Different types of cell make up different body parts. Human body cells include:

- muscle cells
- brain cells
- skin cells
- blood cells

and many more!

HUMAN CELLS: PAGE 36

ANIMALS: PAGE 20

PHOTOSYNTHESIS: PAGE 54

Plant cells

Plants cells are more rigid, and often have a box-like or rectangular shape.

Chloroplasts are special organelles in which photosynthesis happens (making food using light energy).

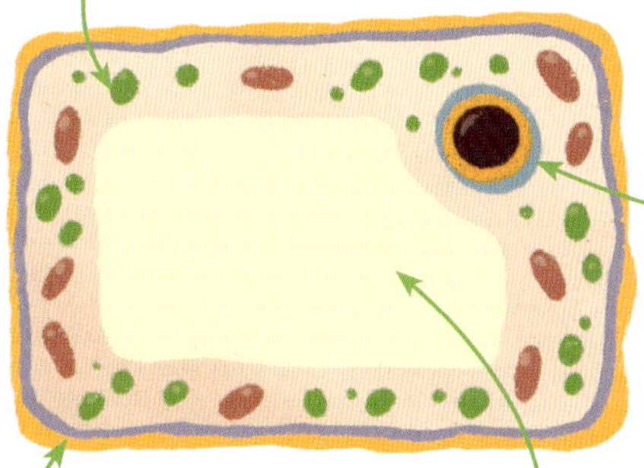

Around the cell membrane is a strong cell wall.

The vacuole is a large space that can fill up with water.

When you water a plant ...

- The vacuoles in its cells fill with liquid.
- The plant is held upright.

When vacuoles are not full, the plant droops.

TYPES OF PLANTS: PAGE 56

Single-celled living things

Microscopic, single-celled creatures live in water, in soil, and in and on other living things. They include:

1. Bacteria and archaea

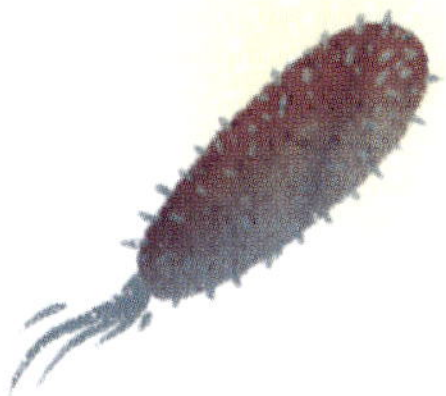

Bacteria—small, simple cells with no cell nucleus.

2. Protists

Single-celled algae—these use sunlight for food, just like plants.

Yeast cells—a type of fungi that takes food from its environment.

MICRO-ORGANISMS: PAGE 70

Genes and DNA

Genes and DNA are incredibly important in biology. They are the parts that control how cells work. They influence how a living thing looks, grows, works, and lives.

Genes and DNA are found inside cells. In cells with a nucleus, they are inside the nucleus. In cells with no nucleus, such as bacteria cells, they float around inside the cell.

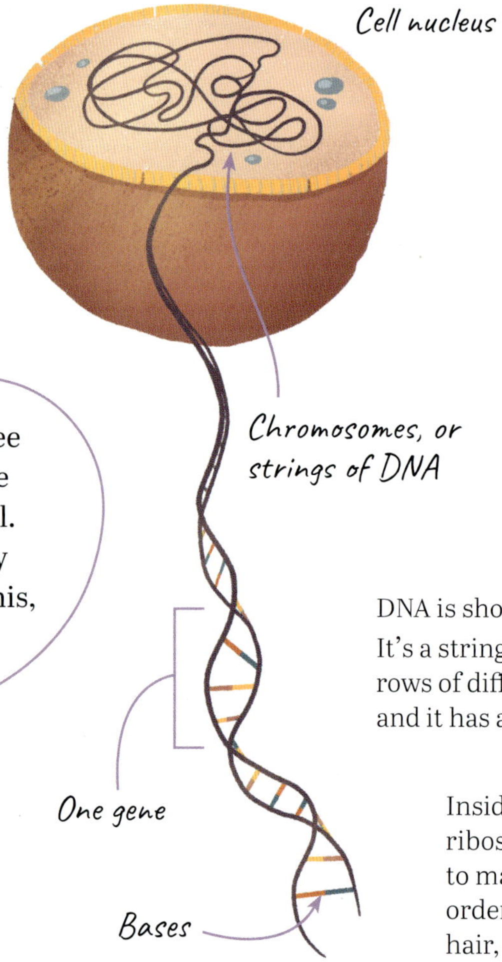

Genes are sections of DNA. Each gene has a particular sequence of bases. They act as instructions, telling cells how to do different jobs.

In this picture you can see a string of DNA from the nucleus of an animal cell. Each cell contains many long strings of DNA like this, called chromosomes.

DNA is short for DeoxyriboNucleic Acid. It's a string-shaped substance made up of rows of different chemicals called bases, and it has a spiral ladder shape.

CELLS: PAGE 10

Inside cells, special organelles called ribosomes follow the instructions in genes to make chemicals that the body needs in order to do different jobs, such as growing hair, making new cells, or making babies.

DNA testing

Since the 1980s, scientists have been able to map, or "sequence," genes and DNA from the cells of living things. This can be very useful.

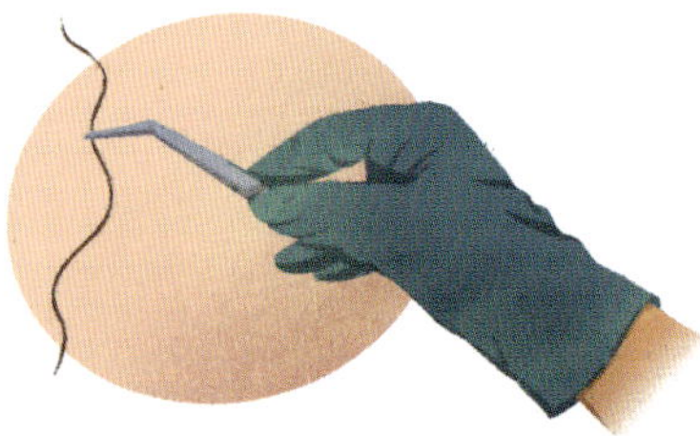

DNA fingerprinting can match cells found at a crime scene to a suspect.

We can test DNA patterns to see how closely related two people are.

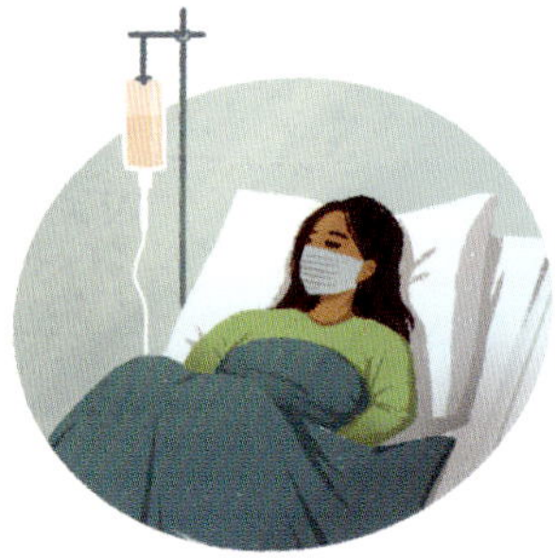

DNA testing can also help to detect and treat some diseases.

HEALTH: PAGE 50

How genes work

Each gene contains the instructions for making a substance—for example, keratin, which is used to grow hair and fingernails.

First, the cell finds the gene it needs in its DNA, and makes a copy of it. Then a ribosome moves along the copy, reading the pattern of bases. Following the instructions, it collects the ingredients it needs to make the keratin.

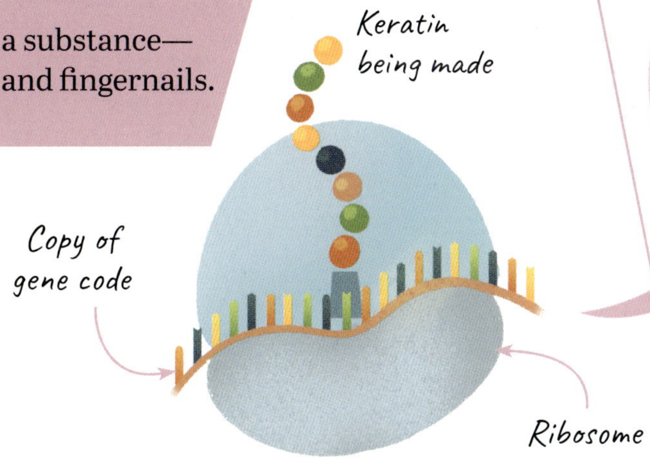

HUMAN CELLS: PAGE 36

Unique patterns

All living things have the same basic system of genes and DNA in their cells. But each species has its own unique set of chromosomes and genes, called its genome.

That's what makes each species the way it is! Its body shape and body parts, and the way it grows, lives, and survives, are decided by the instructions in its genes.

A seahorse's genome makes it grow its horse-like head, curling tail, and fins and gills that allow it to breathe underwater.

A rose's genome makes it grow thorns and sweet-smelling flowers, and leaves that can take in sunshine energy to make food.

PHOTOSYNTHESIS: PAGE 54

Passing it on

When living things reproduce, or have babies, they pass on a copy of their genome to the next generation.

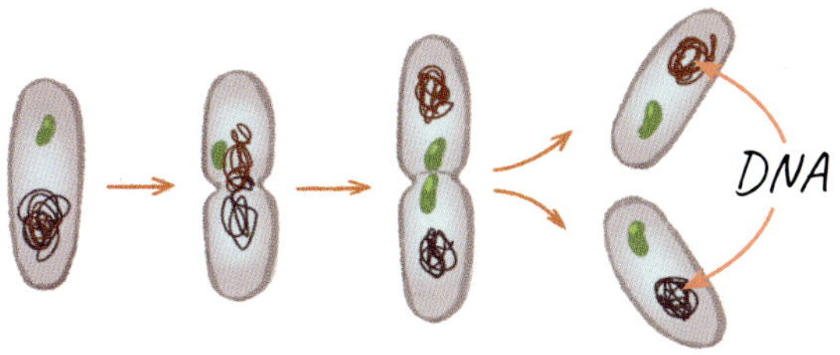

When bacteria cells divide, each new cell gets a copy of the bacteria's DNA.

In mammals, such as cats, two parents pass on a mixture of genes to their babies.

That's why cats have kittens, baby turtles hatch from turtle eggs, and apple seeds grow into apple trees!

ANIMAL LIFE CYCLES: PAGE 32

SEEDS: PAGE 58

Classification

Classification means sorting living things into different groups and types. Biologists do this to show how living things are related to each other, and to identify which groups each species belongs to.

There are several different sorting systems for living things. The one shown here divides species into six kingdoms, or large groups. Each kingdom is divided into smaller families and types.

This classification system can be shown as a "tree of life," with bigger and smaller branches.

Animal kingdom

Vertebrates:

- Mammals
- Birds
- Fish
- Reptiles
- Amphibians

Invertebrates:

- Arthropods
- Mollusks
- Echinoderms
- Worms

The classification tree is always changing as biologists discover, add, and name new species, or change the way that existing ones are classified.

Plant kingdom

- Flowering plants and trees
- Conifers
- Ferns
- Mosses

Fungi kingdom

- Mushrooms and toadstools
- Moulds
- Yeasts

Bacteria kingdom

- Bacteria

Protist kingdom

Single-celled living things, such as:

- Algae
- Amoeba
- Protozoa

Archaea kingdom

- Archaea (similar to bacteria)

Classification pyramids

Each individual species belongs to a kingdom, and to smaller and smaller groups within that kingdom. This can be shown as an upside-down pyramid. Here's the pyramid for the giant metallic stick insect from Madagascar.

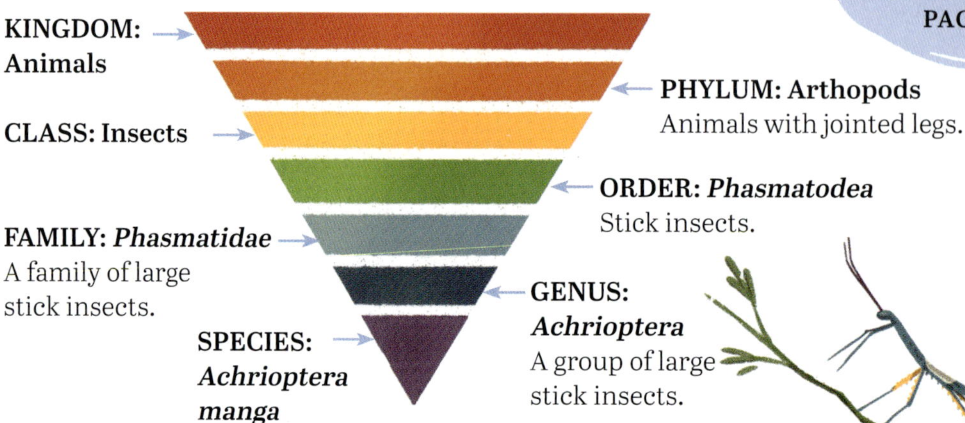

INSECTS: PAGE 24

Where does it belong?

Biologists often discover new species, previously unknown to science—especially smaller ones, like bugs and bacteria. When they do, they have to decide how to classify them.

Biologists can use a living thing's body features, shape, and abilities to help classify it. For example, only birds have feathers and beaks, so if it has these, it's a bird!

The Wakatobi sunbird—a new species discovered in 2022.

If it's hard to be sure, they may test the living thing's DNA. This is useful for microorganisms, such as bacteria.

BIRDS: PAGE 23

MICRO-ORGANISMS: PAGE 70

Species names

Biologists also give each species of the living thing its own scientific name. Species names have two parts and are written in Latin. This means that biologists all over the world, whichever language they speak, can use the same name to talk about a species.

Scientific species names often describe the species in some way, or include the name of whoever discovered it, or sometimes someone famous.

*This flower's Latin name is **Cosmos sulphureus**.*

Cosmos means "orderly," as it has neat, orderly petals.

Sulphureus means it's orangey-yellow, like the element sulphur.

*This lizard was named **Platysaurus attenboroughi** for the famous naturalist Sir David Attenborough.*

Meaning "flat lizard."

Meaning "Attenborough's."

FLOWERS: PAGE 58

REPTILES: PAGE 23

Making changes

Biologists also change the whole classification system to make it work better, or to create new categories.

Until the 1960s, fungi, such as mushrooms, were included in the plant kingdom. In 1969, they got their own, separate kingdom when biologists found they live in a very different way to plants.

Plants make food using sunlight.

Fungi absorb food from what they grow on or in, such as a rotting log.

Common bonnet mushrooms.

PHOTOSYNTHESIS: PAGE 54

FUNGI: PAGE 64

The story of life

Living things have not always existed on planet Earth. For hundreds of millions of years after the world first formed, about 4.54 billion years ago, it was just a barren ball of rock. So how and why did the first life begin? No one knows for sure, but biologists have come up with some theories.

As far as we know, all life on Earth needs water to survive, so biologists think the first life probably began in water, or maybe in warm, wet mud. This is thought to have happened around 4 billion (4 thousand million) years ago.

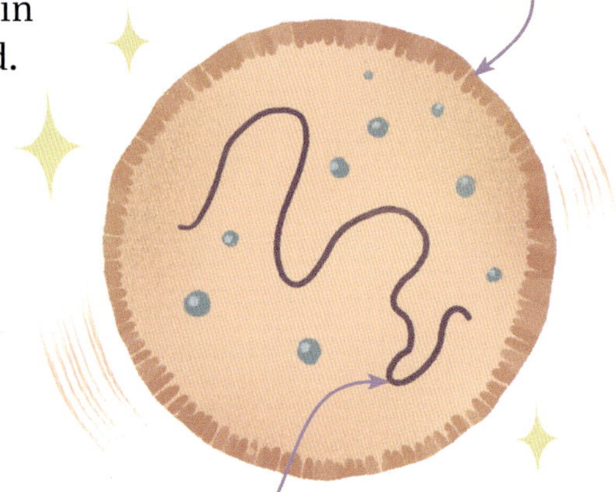

How could life start as a single cell and end up as all the different species alive today? This happened because of evolution—the way life can change over time.

The first life could have formed when chemicals mixed and joined together, perhaps using energy from lightning. It was probably a basic cell with the ability to copy itself.

MICROORGANISMS: PAGE 70

Meet your ancestor!

Scientists think that all living things that exist today, or that have ever existed, developed from one single-celled early life form. No one knows when it existed, but biologists have given it a name: LUCA. It stands for Last Universal Common Ancestor.

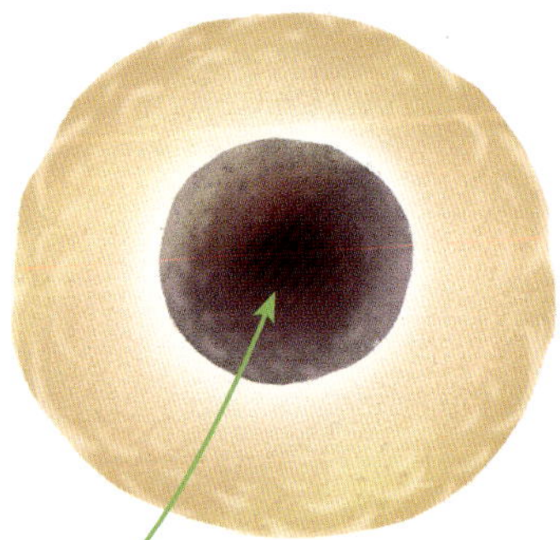

MORE

We're all related!

If all life is descended from LUCA, that explains why all living things have DNA, and use it in the same way. LUCA would have had DNA, and passed it on to all later life forms. This means all living things are related and are one big family!

All living things are your relatives, including cabbages, beetles, and jellyfish.

GENES AND DNA: PAGE 12

Evolution

Whenever living things reproduce, or make new cells, they make a copy of their DNA. Sometimes there's a mistake in the copy that slightly changes the DNA. This can make the new cell different too. Over time, small changes like these can make a species change.

ANIMALS:
PAGE 20

1. Here is an example. This snake species lives in a grassland. Its green skin gives it camouflage. But when the climate changes, the grassland becomes a scrubby desert.

2. Now that the green snakes are easier to see, they mostly get eaten by hawks. Thanks to DNA changes, a few of the snakes are speckled or yellowish.

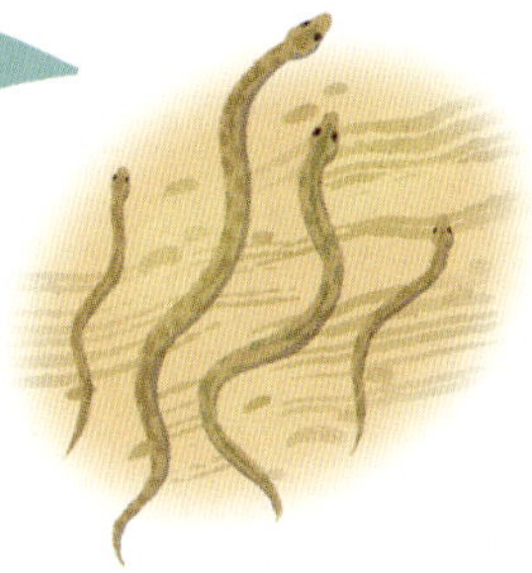

3. The yellowish and speckled snakes mostly survive because they are well camouflaged in the desert. They have more babies and pass on their attributes to them.

4. The species gradually changes to become mostly yellow and speckled, to suit the habitat. This process is called natural selection.

Pick me!

Species can also evolve another way—by being the best at getting a mate. That means they will have more babies and pass on their DNA to them.

Male fiddler crabs have one extra-large claw that they wave to impress females.

INVERTEBRATES:
PAGE 24

Females are attracted to the males with the biggest claws.

Male fiddler crab

ANIMAL LIFE
CYCLES:
PAGE 32

New species

As well as species changing over time, one can branch off from another and become a new species. For example, if some grassland survived and some green snakes stayed there, the desert snakes could eventually become a separate species.

Green grassland snake

Yellow speckled desert snake

Gone forever

If all the members of a species die, it becomes "extinct" and no longer exists. This has happened many times in Earth's history.

Pterodactyls lived millions of years ago and are now extinct.

Prehistoric life

The living things on Earth today are just a tiny fraction—less than 1 percent—of all the species that have ever existed. Many millions of species have evolved and died out in the past. The study of extinct, prehistoric life is called paleontology.

Since life began, it has evolved over billions of years, with species gradually changing and new ones developing.

Some past life forms were unlike any alive today. But others show how today's living things, such as horses or humans, evolved from similar earlier creatures.

How do we know what prehistoric life was like? From fossils and other preserved remains, such as living things that were preserved by being frozen in ice.

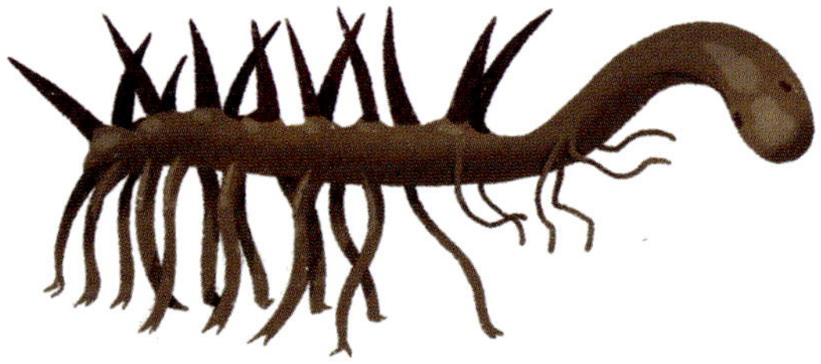

Hallucigenia, a small worm-like animal with legs and spines, lived 508 million years ago.

Over 50 million years, modern horses evolved from a much smaller species called Eohippus.

Life has existed for around 4 billion years. Over that time, it evolved from simple single-celled microorganisms to multi-celled life like fish, trees, dinosaurs, and mammals, including humans.

ANIMALS:
PAGE 20

What is a fossil?

A fossil is a leftover shape or imprint of a living thing, preserved in stone. Fossils usually form when a living thing's body—or the hard parts such as bones—get covered in sand or mud, which eventually hardens into stone. Minerals slowly replace or fill in the shape, making a stony version of it.

Wingspan is 70 cm (27.5 in).

A fossil of Meganeura, a giant insect that lived 300 million years ago.

Trace fossils such as footprints can also reveal clues about prehistoric life.

INSECTS:
PAGE 24

Single-celled life

For billions of years, only simple, single-celled life forms existed.

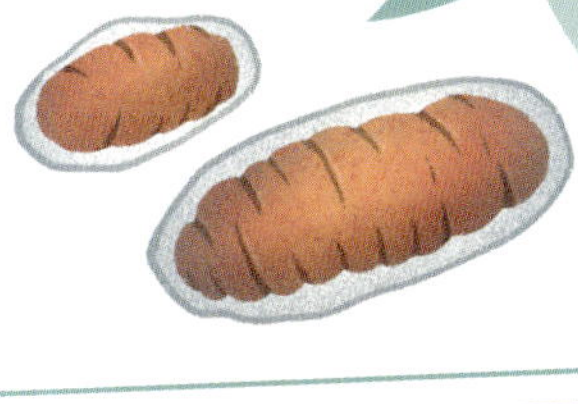

Most early life was similar to present-day bacteria.

BACTERIA: PAGE 70

Multi-celled life

The first life with more than one cell evolved about 600 million years ago.

Anomalocaris was an early relative of today's shrimps.

Life on land

By 400 million years ago, some plants and small animals lived on land.

The first land animals were probably millipedes and their relatives.

ANIMALS: PAGE 20

Dinosaur age

About 240 million years ago, early land reptiles evolved into dinosaurs.

Spinosaurus, a large fish-eating dinosaur.

Rise of the mammals

After the last dinosaurs died out 66 million years ago, many new mammal species evolved.

Elasmotherium was a type of giant rhino.

Elasmotherium

ANIMALS: PAGE 20

Early humans

The first humans only appeared around 2 million years ago.

Homo habilis was an early human species.

HUMANS: PAGE 36

Geological time

The extremely long time since the Earth formed is known as geological time or "deep time." Paleontologists divide it into sections called eons, eras, and periods.

4600 mya

HADEAN EON — No life

4000 mya

ARCHAEAN EON — First life

2500 mya

PROTOREZOIC EON

550 mya

PHANEROZOIC EON:

- Paleozoic Era
  - Cambrian Period
  - Ordovician Period
  - Silurian Period
  - Devonian Period
  - Carboniferous Period
  - Permian Period

250 mya

- Mesozoic Era
  - Triassic Period
  - Jurassic Period
  - Cretaceous Period

66 mya

- Cenozoic Era
  - Tertiary Period
  - Quaternary Period

0 mya

What is an animal?

Animals are a kingdom, or main group, of living things. They include cats and dogs, birds and fish, creepy-crawlies like insects and spiders, and many more. They're probably the most familiar type of living thing to us humans, because we're animals too!

So far, biologists have discovered and named over 1.5 million different species of animals, from tiny worms and tardigrades to huge blue whales. Of the 1.5 million species, over a million are insects! There are more small animal species in the world than big ones.

Birds have their own class, or large group.

Humans belong to the primate group of animals, along with orangutans and other apes, as well as monkeys and lemurs.

Butterflies belong to the insect class of animals.

Dogs and cats are carnivores, or meat-eaters.

The word "animal" comes from a Latin word meaning "breath." Animals breathe in oxygen from the air or water around them, and use it to turn food into energy for their cells.

As well as breathing oxygen, animals have several other key features. They eat food, and usually have a mouth. Most animals move around to find food, at least for part of their lives. And animals are also the only living things to have brains—as far as we know! The study of animals is called zoology.

CELLS: PAGE 10

Animal science

Zoology can be a difficult type of biology to do, as animals are often good at hiding, running, swimming, or flying away. Some can be dangerous too, such as venomous spiders or snakes, and fierce tigers. And because many animals can think and feel pain, zoologists have to be careful to treat them well.

Zoologists sometimes need special skills, such as climbing, scuba diving, or caving, to find and observe animals.

BIOLOGISTS: PAGE 8

On the move

Animals have evolved several different ways of getting around, including walking and running, hopping and jumping, swimming, flying, slithering and crawling, and even rolling.

Bats, most birds, and some insects can fly.

Pearl moth caterpillars make a wheel shape and roll away to escape from danger.

INVERTEBRATES: PAGE 24

Fish, squid, and penguins can swim underwater.

Many animals walk or run on two, four, six, or more legs.

VERTEBRATES: PAGE 26

Finding food

To grow and survive, animals have to feed on other living things. This means they have to find, hunt, catch, or collect food from their surroundings. For example, wolves hunt and eat deer, while deer move around to eat plants and fungi.

Biologists use different words to describe animals, depending on what they eat.

- **Carrnivores** eat meat.
- **Herbivores** eat plants.
- **Fungivores** eat fungi.
- **Omnivores** eat a variety of foods including meat and plants.
- **Scavengers** eat decaying, dead animals and plants, or waste such as animal poop.

Dung beetles are scavengers. They collect balls of animal poop to feed their babies.

LIFE CYCLES: PAGE 32

Super-smart

Not all animals have a brain—for example, jellyfish and sea anemones manage without one. But most animals do, and some are clever enough to solve problems, invent new hunting methods, or even learn human words. Most animals also have eyes, ears, and other sense organs.

DOLPHINS: PAGE 31

Orcas are highly intelligent sea mammals. They have big brains and talk to each other using a range of sounds.

Types of animals

The 1.5 million known animal species are divided into groups based on the way they live, breathe, and feed; their body features and shapes; and their abilities, such as a spider's ability to spin silk.

CLASSIFICATION: PAGE 14

On these two pages, you can see the main animal groups, and the typical features and abilities that each group has.

There are two main groups of animals:

- Invertebrates
- Vertebrates

Within each of these are more, smaller groups.

INVERTEBRATES: PAGE 24

Invertebrates

Invertebrates get their name because they don't have vertebrae—in other words, no backbone. Instead, some have a tough outer covering called an exoskeleton. Others have soft bodies that use the pressure of liquid inside them to keep their shape.

Arthropods

Arthropods have jointed legs, and often a hard, protective skin or exoskeleton. They include ...

Insects

- Arachnids, such as spiders and scorpions
- Crustaceans, such as crabs and shrimps
- Myriapods, like millipedes and centipedes

Worms

There are many different types of worms, in three main groups:

- Flatworms
- Roundworms
- Segmented worms, such as earthworms

Cnidarians

These animals all live in water and have jelly-like bodies, sometimes with tentacles.

- Jellyfish
- Sea anemones
- Corals
- Hydrozoa, such as the Portuguese man-o-war

Mollusks

These animals have soft bodies, with or without shells, and many of them live in water.

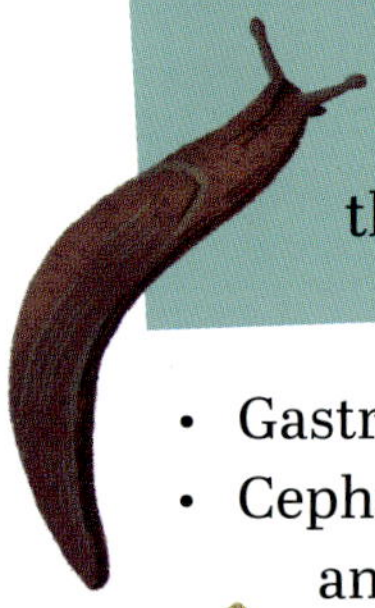

- Gastropods, or slugs and snails
- Cephalopods, like octopuses and squid
- Bivalves, or two-shelled sea creatures, such as mussels

Echinoderms

Echinoderms are unusual, as their bodies are made up of five equal sections.

- Sea stars
- Sea cucumbers
- Sea urchins

Vertebrates

Vertebrates are animals with vertebrae, or backbones. They usually have a skeleton made up of bones linked together by moving joints.

VERTEBRATES: PAGE 26

Fish

Fish were the first vertebrates to evolve, and all other vertebrates developed from them. They breathe underwater and swim using their fins and tails.

- Bony fish, such as cod and clownfish
- Sharks and rays

EVOLUTION: PAGE 17

Amphibians

These animals lay their eggs in water but can also breathe air as adults.

- Frogs and toads
- Salamanders
- Newts

Birds

Birds evolved from a type of dinosaur and are dinosaurs' closest living relatives. They have two legs, two wings, feathers, and beaks—and most can fly.

- Birds of prey
- Water birds
- Songbirds and perching birds
- Flightless birds, such as the ostrich

Reptiles

Unlike amphibians, reptiles only breathe air. They often have scaly skin.

- Crocodiles and alligators
- Tortoises and turtles
- Snakes
- Lizards

Mammals

Like birds, mammals are warm-blooded, so they can stay warmer than their surroundings. Mother mammals feed their babies on milk from their bodies.

- Carnivores, such as wolves and tigers
- Ungulates, or hoofed mammals
- Rodents, like mice and squirrels
- Primates, like monkeys and apes
- Bats
- Cetaceans (whales and dolphins)
- Pinnipeds, such as seals
- Proboscids, such as elephants
- Marsupials, such as kangaroos
- Monotremes, such as the platypus

HUNTING: PAGE 29

Humans

Humans are mammals and evolved from chimpanzee-like animals. We have unusually big brains, are good at inventing and making things, and use language.

HUMANS: PAGE 36

Invertebrates

Invertebrates, or animals without backbones, make up 97 percent of all animal species. Although some of them, such as cockroaches and slugs, are seen as pests or a nuisance, invertebrates are also very important.

As well as many different species, there are huge numbers of invertebrates themselves. For example, biologists estimate that there are around 20 quadrillion (20,000,000,000,000,000) ants on Earth!

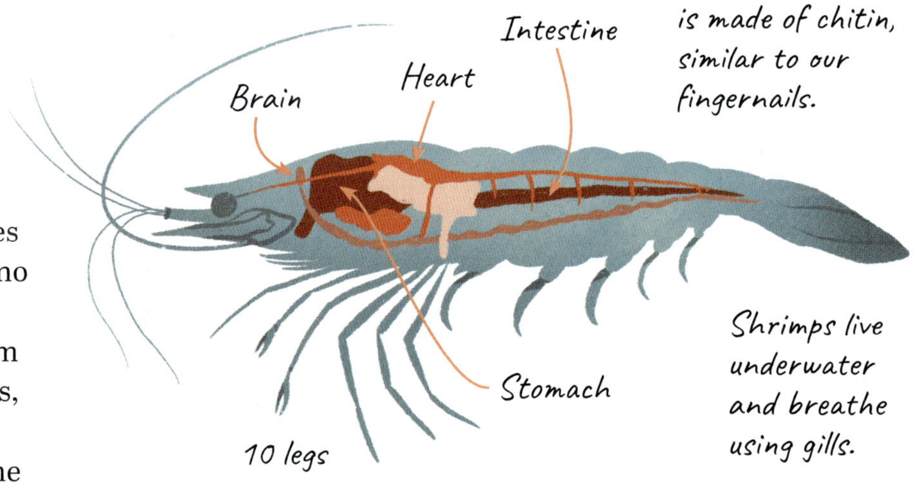

Invertebrates either have no legs, or lots of legs—from six in insects, up to over 1,000 in some millipedes.

This shrimp is an invertebrate. It's small, with a hard outer covering, or exoskeleton, and 10 legs.

Invertebrates may be mostly small, but they have many ways to find food and protect themselves, making them super-survivors!

Incredible insects

Insects are the biggest group of invertebrates, with over a million species. They live in land and freshwater habitats. There are many types, including ants, bees, butterflies and moths, flies, fleas, grasshoppers, bugs, and beetles. There are over 400,000 species of beetles!

Is it an insect?

Though they come in many types and shapes, all insects have the same basic body plan:

EVOLUTION: PAGE 17

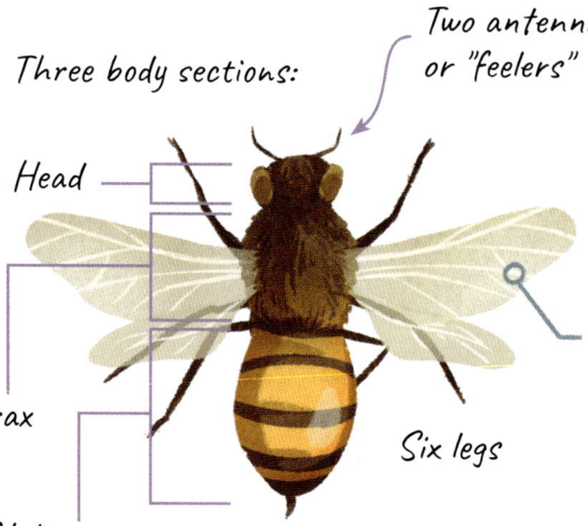

Insects were the first animals to evolve flight, around 400 million years ago.

HABITATS: PAGE 76

How big can they be?

Most invertebrates are small because it's hard to hold up a big body without the framework of a bony skeleton.

In the sea, the water supports animals' bodies, so invertebrates can grow bigger. The giant squid is one of the biggest—including its tentacles, it can be over 10 m (33 ft) long.

However, being small can have advantages. Small animals can grow fast and can reproduce quickly.

Little black ants are only about 2 mm (.08 in) long.

FOOD: PAGE 28

Protection

Invertebrates have other ways to stay safe and protect themselves, including shells, stinging, and biting.

The Brazilian wandering spider has a venomous bite.

Lots of sea molluscks have thick, strong shells to protect them from danger. The animal builds the shell using minerals that it takes in from the seawater.

Cone snails shoot a harpoon into their enemies, delivering deadly venom.

Horseshoe crabs hide under their wide, dish-shaped shells.

Important invertebrates

Invertbrates are very important to other living things, including humans, in both helpful and harmful ways.

HELPFUL:

- Pollinating plants.
- Providing food for other animals, such as birds and bats.
- Cleaning up waste by eating poop and dead animals.
- Burrowing through soil and making it more fertile.

HARMFUL:

- Biting other animals, sucking our blood, and sometimes spreading diseases.
- Eating our crops and food stores.

GERMS AND DISEASES: PAGE 72

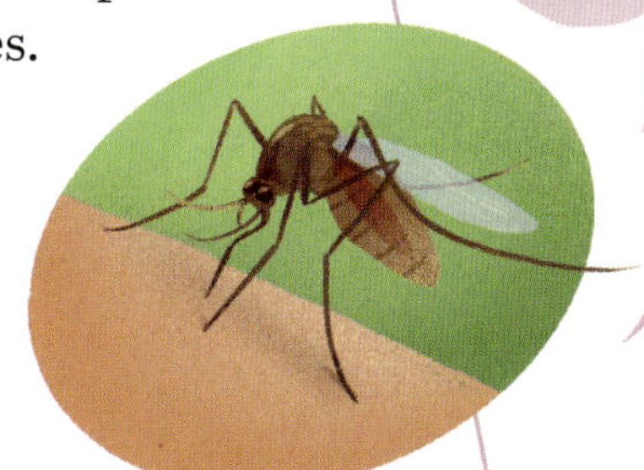

Mosquitos can spread diseases such as malaria.

POLLINATION: PAGE 58

Vertebrates

There are about 60,000 species of vertebrate animals—far fewer than there are invertebrates. However, these animals are often bigger and more noticeable. They include fish, amphibians, reptiles, birds, and mammals, such as cats, dogs, elephants, and humans.

Vertebrates have vertebrae, or backbones. You can feel your own backbone easily—it's the row of bumpy bones down the middle of your back. The backbone is the central part of a vertebrate's skeleton, linking the other main parts together.

Vertebrates' backbones, and the rest of their skeletons, are mostly made from hard bones that contain minerals. Some parts (such as the tip of your nose) are made from more rubbery, flexible cartilage.

Vertbrates are all closely related, as they all evolved from fish, the first vertebrates. This means the same basic body parts have been passed on in the genes, and can be found in all vertebrates.

GENES AND DNA: PAGE 12

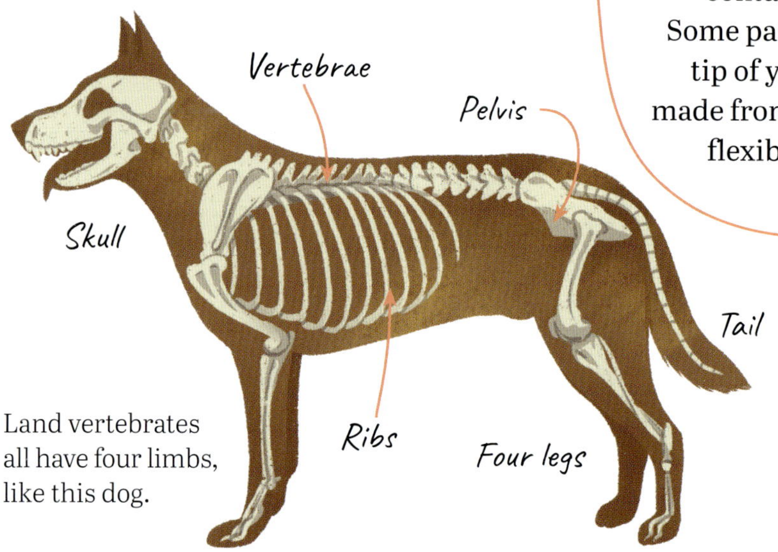

Land vertebrates all have four limbs, like this dog.

Matching skeletons

If you look at vertebrate skeletons, you can see that they all have the same basic structure, even in different groups such as birds and mammals. The backbone links the skull to the pelvis or tail, and there are up to four limbs.

Though they have evolved into different shapes, all the skeletons have a backbone, a skull, ribs, and fins or limbs.

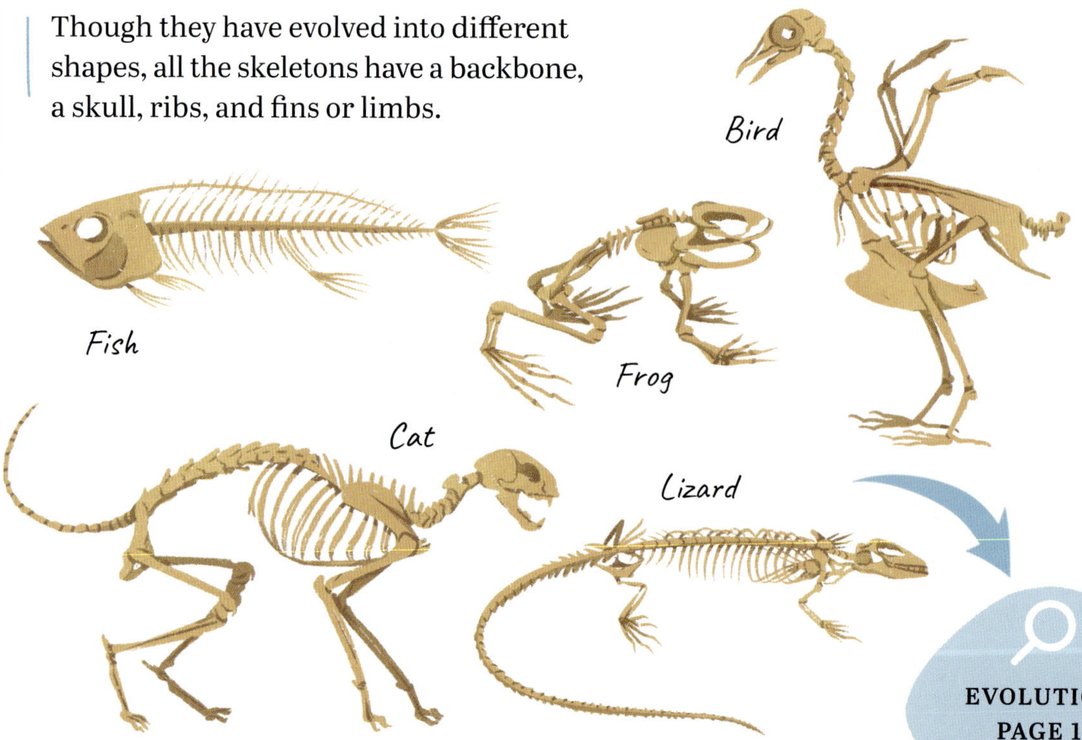

EVOLUTION: PAGE 17

Vertebrate tails

The tail in a vertebrate extends from the backbone. Some species have lost their tails as they evolved over time, but many still have them.

Apes and monkeys are closely related, but most monkeys have tails, while apes, including humans, have lost them over years of evolution.

Some monkeys use their tails like limbs to hold branches. They're called prehensile tails.

Spider monkey

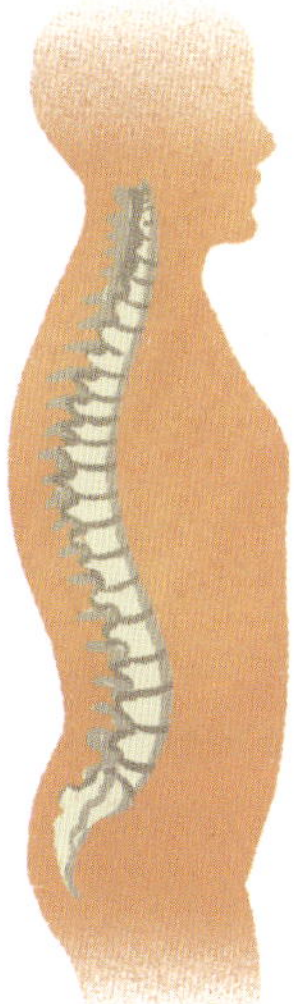

Human tailbone

Humans don't have tails, but we do have a short "tailbone" at the end of the backbone.

HUMAN SKELETON: PAGE 38

Mouths and teeth

Like all animals, vertebrates need to eat food. Their mouths and teeth have evolved into different types and shapes, depending on what the animal feeds on or uses its teeth for.

Meat-eaters have sharp teeth for cutting and tearing.

Birds have hard beaks instead of teeth.

Plant-eaters have flatter teeth for grinding.

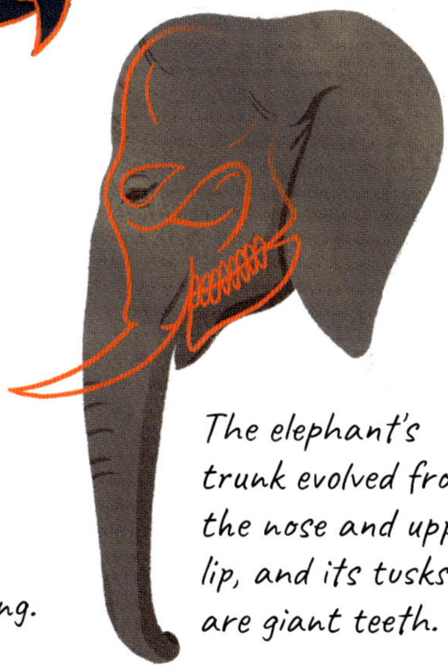

The elephant's trunk evolved from the nose and upper lip, and its tusks are giant teeth.

FOOD: PAGE 28

Limbs or no limbs?

Fish have fins, and most other vertebrates have four limbs in two pairs. Over time, some animals' limbs have evolved into arms, wings, or flippers. Others started off with legs but have now lost them.

Humpback whale

Whales have two flippers.

Birds have two legs and two wings.

Grey heron

Tree boa snake

Snakes evolved from four-legged lizards and lost their legs.

EVOLUTION: PAGE 17

Finding food

Animals spend a lot of their time making sure they get enough to eat—whether they're grazing on grass, feeding on fungi or searching for prey to hunt. And like us, they also need to take in water to stay alive.

Each animal species has its own way of finding food, as well as body parts that help it to collect or catch plants or prey. For example, snakes can stretch their jaws and bodies to swallow animals much wider than they are.

FOOD CHAINS: PAGE 78

Some animals can go without food for days or even weeks, especially desert-dwellers such as camels and snakes. This helps them to survive when food is scarce.

This python has swallowed an antelope.

Pythons swallow their prey whole, then lie still for days while they digest it.

As plants mostly stay still, it's easier for plant-eaters to find food, but they have to eat a lot of plants to get enough energy. Meat-eaters don't need as much food, but it can be harder for them to find and catch prey, so they have a wide range of hunting methods, tricks, and traps.

Plant-eaters

Herbivores, or plant-eaters, often feed on a particular type of plant or plant part, such as leaves or flower nectar. Some, like squirrels and pikas, store food when they can, so that they have a lasting supply.

Useful features

Animals often evolve features and abilities that help them compete with other species to get more food. For example, giraffes' long necks help them reach higher than other animals to feed on tree leaves.

Hummingbirds can hover in one place and use their long beaks and tongues to collect nectar.

Leafcutter ants bite off pieces of leaf, then carry them to their nest, where they use them to grow a type of fungi that they feed on.

Giraffes reach up into trees and use their long tongues to strip the leaves off.

TREES: PAGE 57

High speed hunters

Lots of hunting animals, such as cheetahs, bats, birds of prey, mako sharks, and leopard seals, rely on chasing and catching their prey by running, flying, or swimming after it.

FISH: PAGE 23

Speedy sharks

Mako sharks are the fastest of all sharks, and can swim at over 50 km/h (31 mi/h). They chase and catch other fast fish such as tuna.

Some hunters, like wolves, work in teams to surround their prey as they chase it down.

Lying in wait

Ambush hunting is a different strategy that uses less energy. The hunter hides and waits for prey to come close, before suddenly grabbing it. Some animals attract the prey with a bait.

Flower mantises are camouflaged to look like flower petals. They sit still and wait, and then catch unwary insects quickly with their front legs.

The alligator snapping turtle hides on riverbeds and opens its mouth to show a part that looks like a worm. Fish swim up to catch the worm and get snapped up!

Special skills

A few animals have evolved unusual abilities to help them hunt.

Clever chimps have worked out how to fish termites out of their nests with a twig.

ANIMAL INTELLIGENCE: PAGE 30

Chameleons shoot their long, sticky tongues out to grab prey.

The nest-casting spider spins a silk net, then uses it to catch its prey.

Animal brains and senses

Of all living things, animals—especially vertebrates—are the smartest and have the most powerful senses. Some animals have senses much more sensitive than ours, or senses we don't have at all.

In most animals, the brain is a very important organ. It receives signals from sense organs, such as eyes and ears, and works out what they mean. It also sends signals to the rest of the body to make it move or do things, such as eat, breathe, and sleep.

Most animals have one brain, which is in their head, like this mouse.

Some have more than one brain!

- Leeches have 32 brains—one for each body segment.
- Cockroaches have two.
- Octopuses have nine: a main brain, and a separate long, skinny brain for each tentacle.

Animal brains range from tiny tardigrade brains smaller than a dot to the biggest, belonging to the sperm whale, which is five times the size of a human brain.

HUMAN BRAIN: PAGE 46

Brainless!

- Sponges, starfish, jellyfish, and sea urchins are among the animals with no brain at all.

Moon jelly

Many animals have the same senses as humans: sight, sound, touch, taste, and smell. But they don't always work the same way. For example, while dogs and cats smell with their noses, insects use their antennae. Some animals have other senses, too, and some are very intelligent.

MORE

Acting on instinct

Animals can do all kinds of amazing things, but this isn't always because they're super-smart. Some actions, like spiders spinning webs and birds building nests, are instincts, meaning they are built into the animal's brain, and it knows how to do them automatically.

EGGS: PAGE 33

Baya weaver birds weave their nests from grass and strips of leaf. There's a long entrance tunnel and a safe shelf inside for the eggs. But this is instinctive, and they don't have to learn how to do it.

Super-senses

We can't imagine what it's like to have the amazing senses some animals have! Eagles have brilliant eyesight to help them spot prey on the ground. Owls and elephants have much more sensitive hearing than humans. Dogs, wolves, and moths have a much better sense of smell.

Some male moths, such as the luna moth, can detect the scent of a female from as far as 10 km (6 mi) away, using their super-sensitive, feathery or fringed antennae.

INSECTS: PAGE 24

LIFE CYCLES: PAGE 32

Extra senses

A few animals can sense things that humans can't, using special sense organs.

- Electroreception and seeing UV or IR light.
- Echolocation.

Snakes can detect heat, given off by warm objects, using pits on their faces.

The blue-spotted ribbontail ray uses its electrical sense to hunt for worms and fish hiding under the seabed sand.

HUNTING: PAGE 29

Cleverest animals

There are several signs of true intelligence that biologists can test for in animals, such as:

- Solving problems
- Inventing things
- Playing games
- Learning from experiences
- Copying other animals or humans.

The smartest animals include chimps, pigs, elephants, crows, dolphins, octopuses, and squid.

Scientists working in a biology aquarium rewarded dolphins for collecting bits of litter from their pool. One smart dolphin, Kelly, figured out how to get extra treats by tearing the litter into smaller pieces!

BIOLOGISTS: PAGE 8

Life cycles

A life cycle is a sequence of changes an animal goes through in its life. It is born, grows up, and then gets old and dies. Animals reproduce, or have babies, so that their species carries on even after they die.

You can show the life cycle of an animal species as a circular diagram, like this:

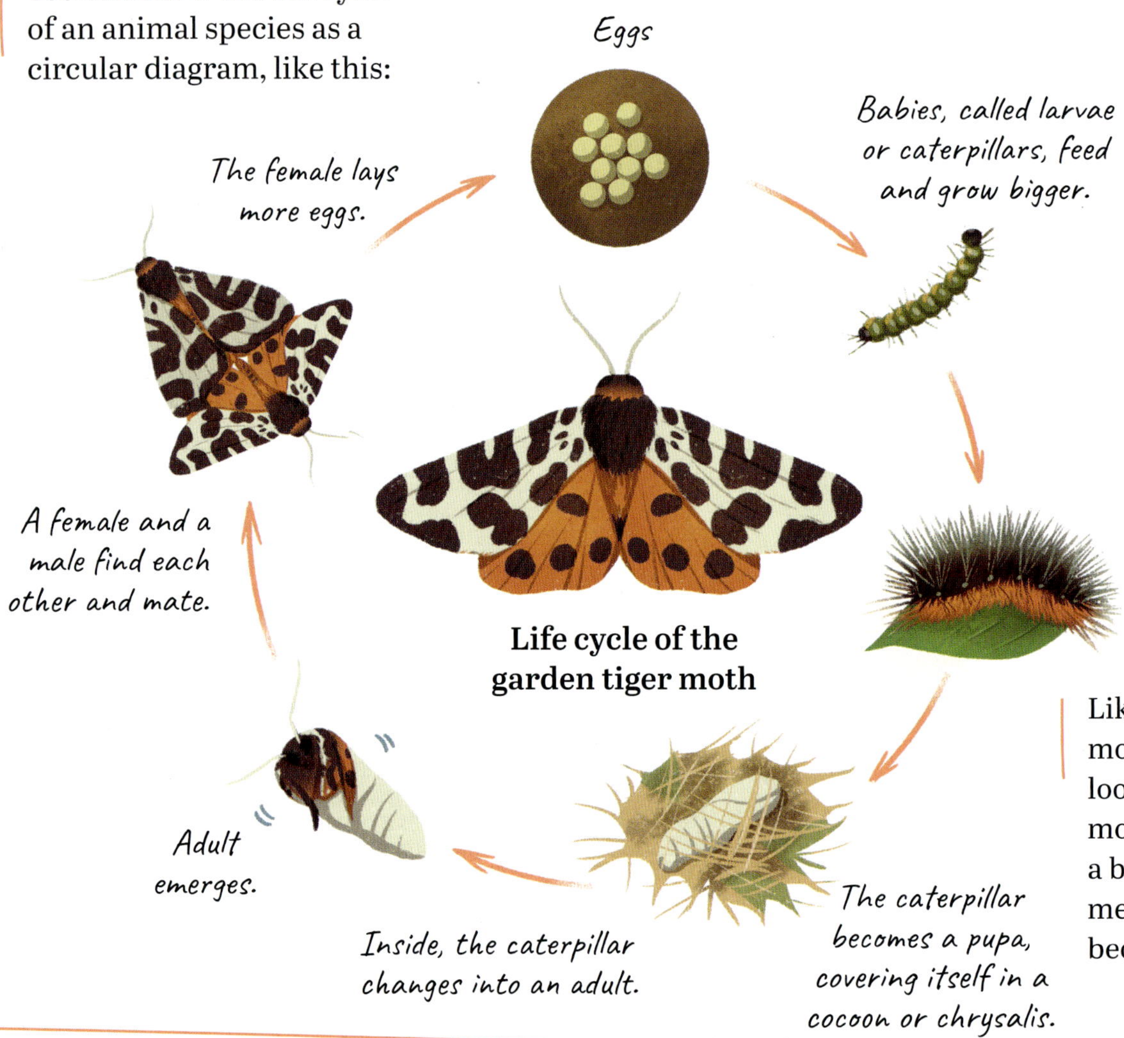

Life cycle of the garden tiger moth

In most species, it takes two adults, a male and a female, to have babies. Others only need one parent. Some lay eggs, while others give birth to live babies.

Like many insects, moth babies do not look like fully grown moths. They go through a big change, called metamorphosis, to become adults.

Meeting and mating

When animals mate, the male gives the female some cells from his body. A male and a female cell combine to make a new cell that can become a baby. Most animals have babies in this way, known as sexual reproduction.

Mute swans can stay with the same partner for years, sometimes until they die.

CELLS: PAGE 10

No mates!

Some animals can reproduce without a mate. This is known as asexual reproduction.

Hydras are water animals that look a bit like tiny trees. They have babies by "budding."

Parent hydra — *A bud grows from the side of the hydra ...* — *It becomes a baby hydra ...* — *... then breaks off and grows into an adult.*

Eggs or no eggs?

Most animals, especially birds, fish, amphibians, and invertebrates, have babies by laying eggs. The baby hatches from the egg after growing inside.

Crocodiles lay their eggs in a riverside nest.

A mother crocodile with her eggs.

REPTILES: PAGE 23

This giraffe has just given birth to her baby.

MAMMALS: PAGE 23

Some animals, including most mammals, give birth to live babies instead.

Parental care

Parental care means looking after babies as they grow. Mammals and birds do this, but not all animals do.

REPTILES: PAGE 23

Mother sea turtles lay their eggs in the sand on a beach and then swim away. When the babies hatch, they have to make their way to the sea to find their own food.

Meerkats care for their babies and teach them how to catch scorpions to eat.

Useful animals

Animals can be useful to humans for their meat, wool, feathers, skins, and more. We can also train them to do work for us, and we keep them as pets.

Humans have been living alongside animals ever since we first evolved, millions of years ago.

This cave painting in Spain shows prehistoric people hunting with bows and arrows.

In prehistoric times, early humans hunted wild animals like deer and mammoths, caught fish, and collected seafood such as clams.

We have bred all kinds of domestic animals for a range of different uses.

Gradually, some humans began farming animals. They chose animals with the most useful qualities to breed from, known as selective breeding. Over time, this created "domestic" farm animals that are different from their wild cousins.

Today's farm cows were bred from wild aurochs, which are now extinct.

Farm animals

Farm animals have been bred to be calmer and often smaller than their wild ancestors, and for their useful qualities, such as thick wool.

Some of the farm animals we keep today:

MAMMALS: PAGE 23

EGGS: PAGE 33

Working animals

Working animals do useful jobs for us. They're usually intelligent species, such as horses, that can be trained to understand humans.

People began domesticating wild horses in eastern Europe and western Asia over 4,000 years ago. Today, we use different breeds of horse for riding and sports, and for pulling carriages, carts, or ploughs.

Police horses can help to control crowds and give police officers a better view.

These can all be working animals too:

- **Dogs**—used to find disaster survivors, guard property, rescue people, and assist people with disabilities.
- **Rats**—used to detect drugs, diseases, and landmines by smell.
- **Pigeons**—used in wartime to carry messages.
- **Yaks, camels, llamas, and donkeys**—used to carry heavy loads.
- **Oxen and buffaloes**—used to pull ploughs.
- **Geese**—used to scare away intruders!

DISEASES: PAGE 72

ANIMAL SENSES: PAGE 30

Pets

Animals can be our friends too—especially dogs and cats.

Dogs were bred from wild wolves thousands of years ago. There are now hundreds of different breeds.

Is it right?

Some people think it's wrong to use animals, especially to kill them for meat or other products. Vegetarians don't eat meat, while vegans don't use any animal products at all, including meat, milk, eggs, leather, feathers, honey, or wool.

Vegans only eat food made from plants.

FOOD: PAGE 28

What is a human?

Humans are a type of mammal. We belong to the primate order—or group—of mammals, and are part of the ape family, along with chimps, gorillas, gibbons, and orangutans.

Like other apes, instead of having four legs, humans have two legs and two arms. We usually move around by walking or running.

Chimps often use their arms to help them walk.

Gibbons mainly swing through trees using their arms.

Some other apes, especially gorillas, can stand upright, but humans do it most of all.

Like other animals' bodies, the human body is made up of tiny cells which form all the different body parts, including tissues like bone and muscle, and organs such as the stomach and brain.

Body cells

The average human body is made up of a mind-boggling 37 trillion cells (that's 37 million million, or 37,000,000,000,000).

There are about 200 different types of cell, found in different body parts. On their own, each cell is microscopic and too small to see.

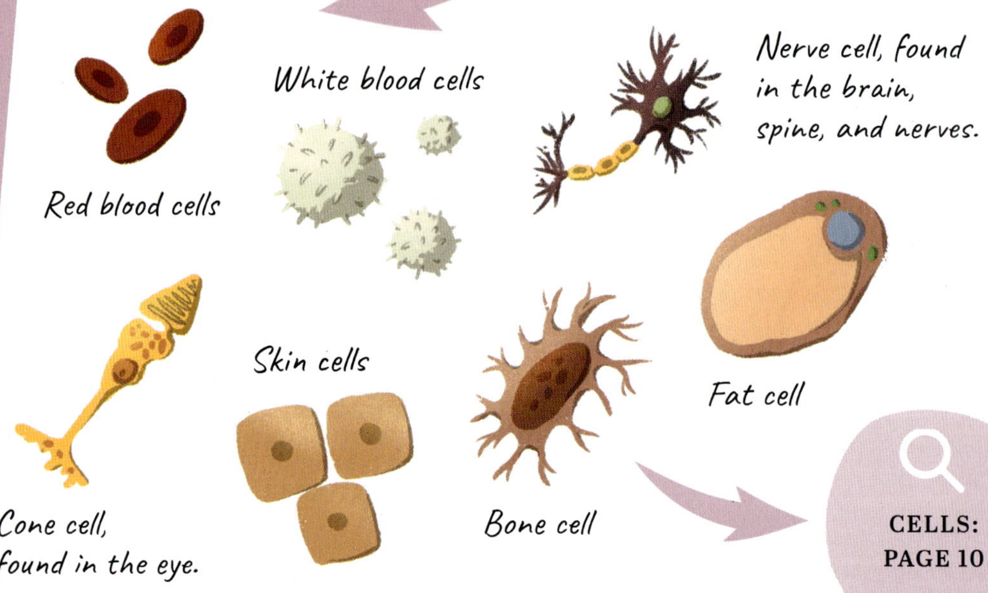

CELLS: PAGE 10

Body organs

Organs are larger body parts that do particular jobs. For example, the brain takes in information, makes decisions and controls the body, and the lungs suck in air and collect oxygen from it.

This picture shows the main body organs.

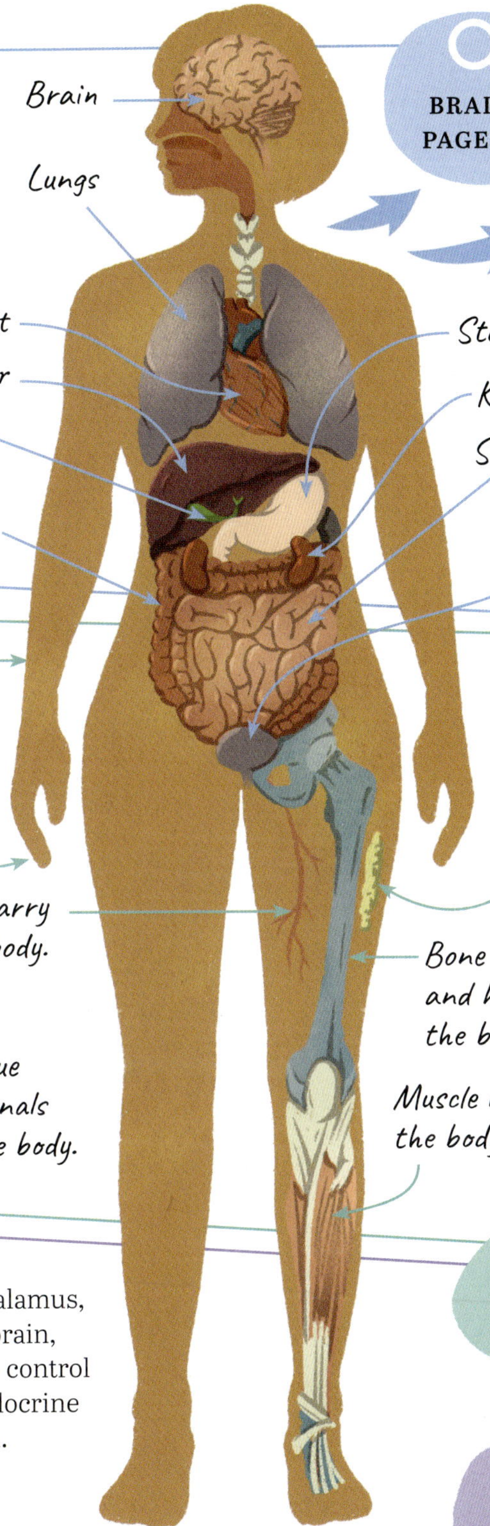

BRAIN: PAGE 46

LUNGS: PAGE 42

Body tissues

Body tissues make up other body parts, such as skin, bone, fat, muscle and hair.

Each body tissue is made of its own special types of cells, and works in its own way.

SKIN: PAGE 44

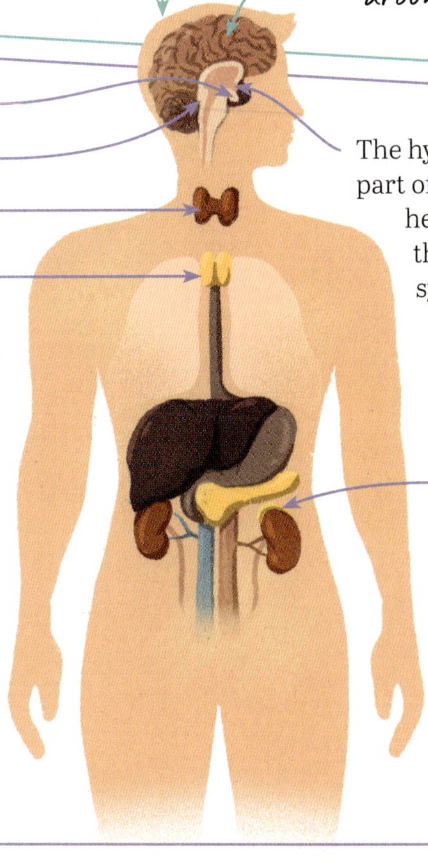

Body systems

Groups of organs and tissues work together as body systems, which help the body to do different things.

BRAIN: PAGE 46

For example, the endocrine system is made of small organs called glands. They release chemicals called hormones that help to control how the body works.

Bones and muscles

Without your bones, you'd be a jelly-like blob on the floor. And without your muscles, you wouldn't be able to move your bones!

Altogether, the human body has 206 bones, and more than 600 skeletal muscles.

These two sets of body parts work together to help you stand, sit up, and move around. Together, they are known as the musculoskeletal system.

Bones are made of bone cells combined with hard minerals, especially calcium.

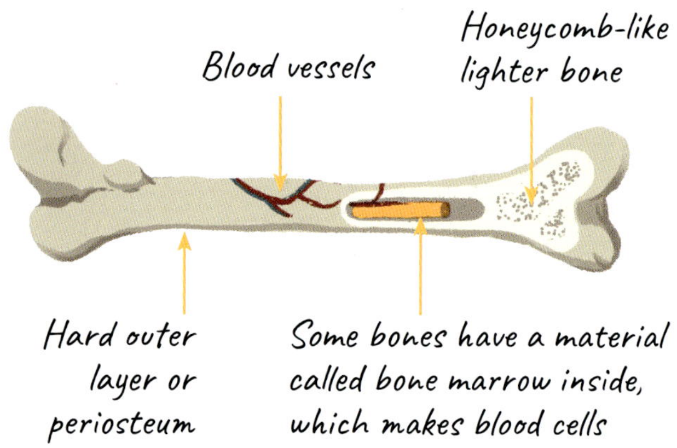

Skeletal muscles are strong, stretchy body parts that attach to bones. They contract, or shorten, to pull on bones and make them move.

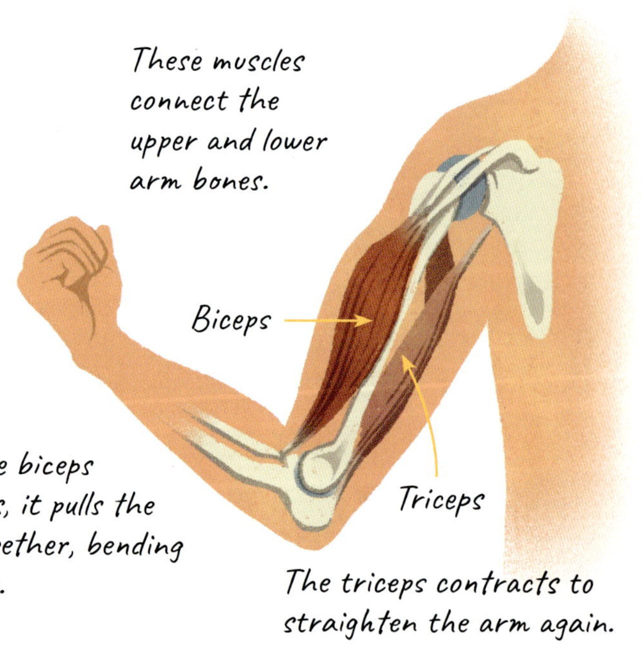

BLOOD VESSELS: PAGE 43

BLOOD CELLS: PAGE 43

Bones of the skeleton

Human bones range in size from the large femur (thigh bone) and pelvis, to three tiny bones in the ear that help you hear.

Most bones have scientific names in Latin, but some also have everyday names.

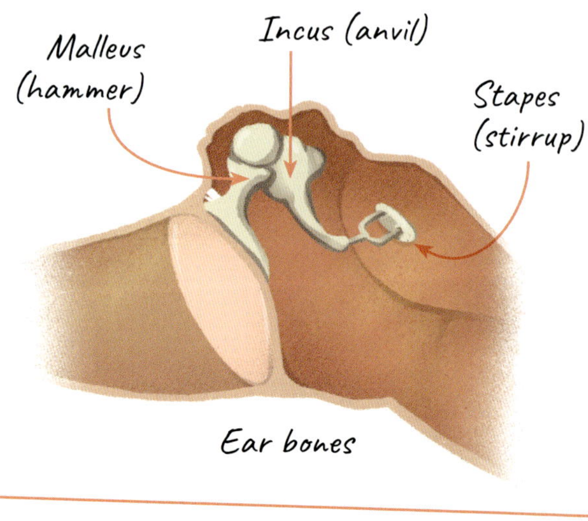

HEARING: PAGE 47

Joints

Bones are linked together by flexible joints, so that they can change position.

Joints link and move bones in several different ways ...

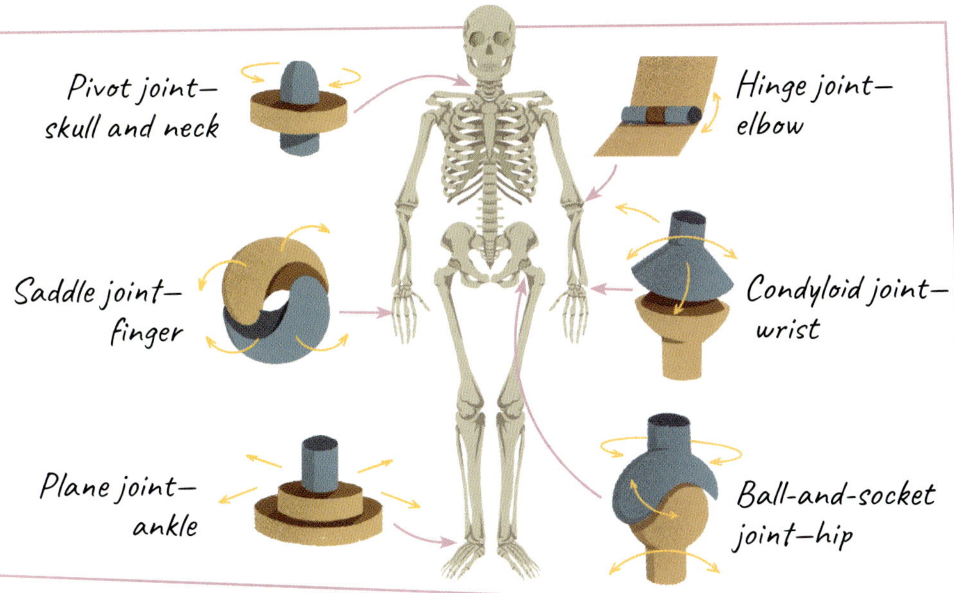

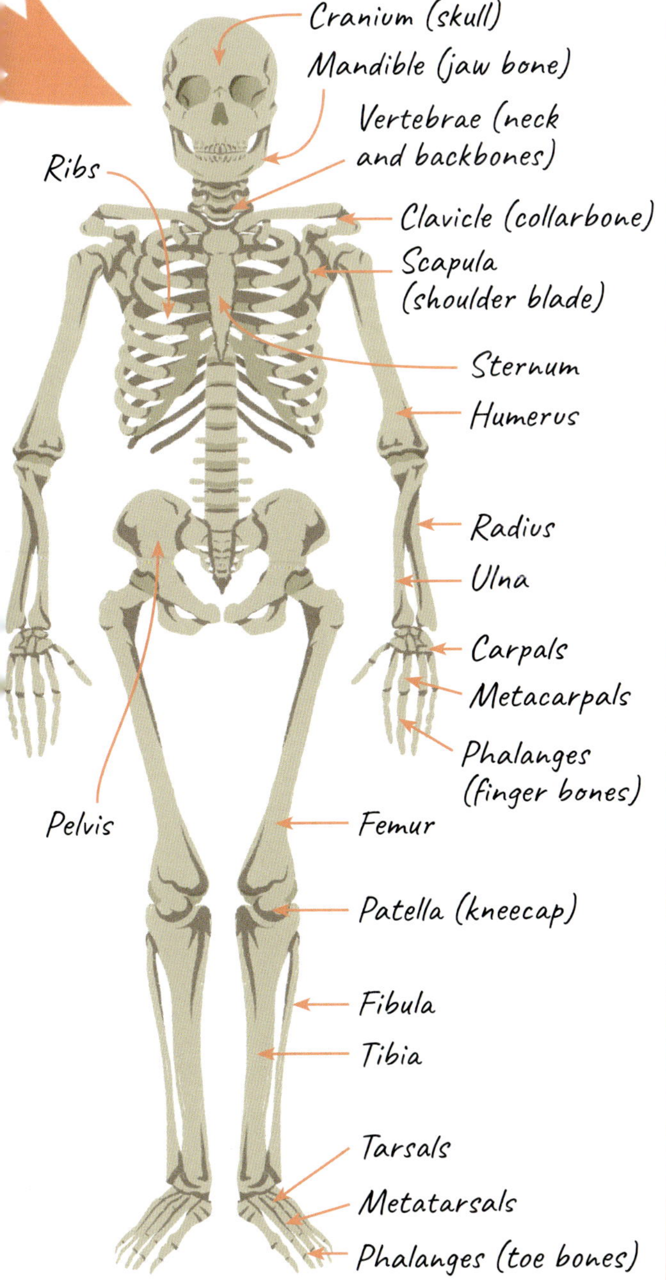

Moving muscles

The skeletal muscles cover most of the skeleton, linking and pulling on all the bones.

Muscles are connected to bones by tough stringy parts called tendons.

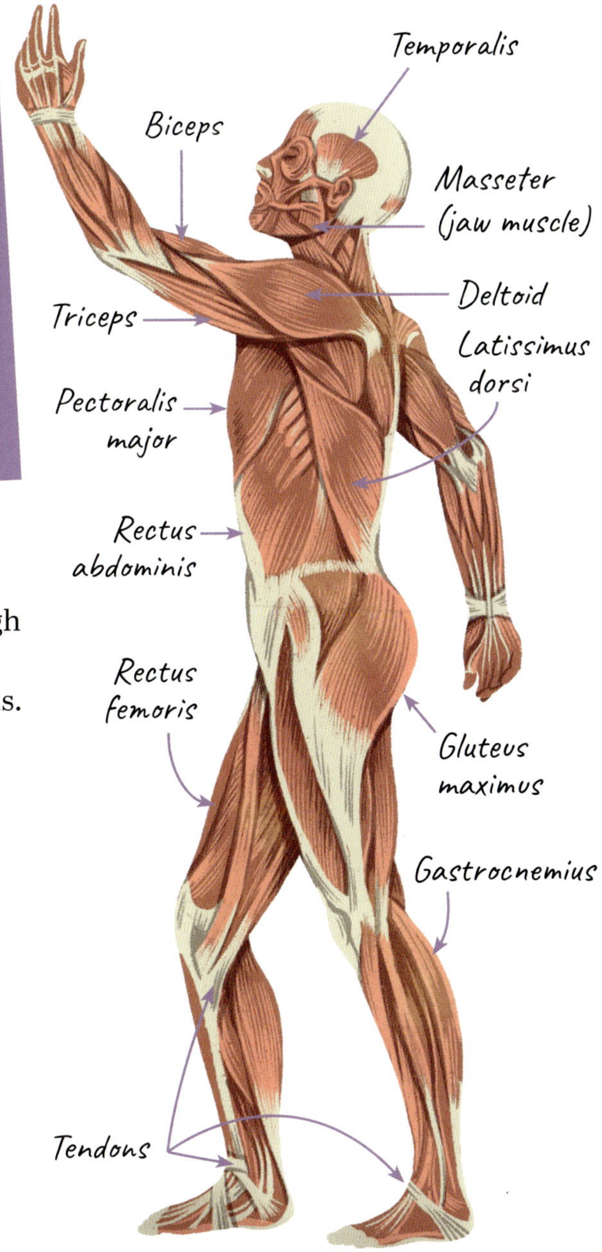

HEALTH:
PAGE 50

The digestive system

The digestive system is the body system that takes in food, and extracts all the useful food chemicals, or nutrients, that the body needs.

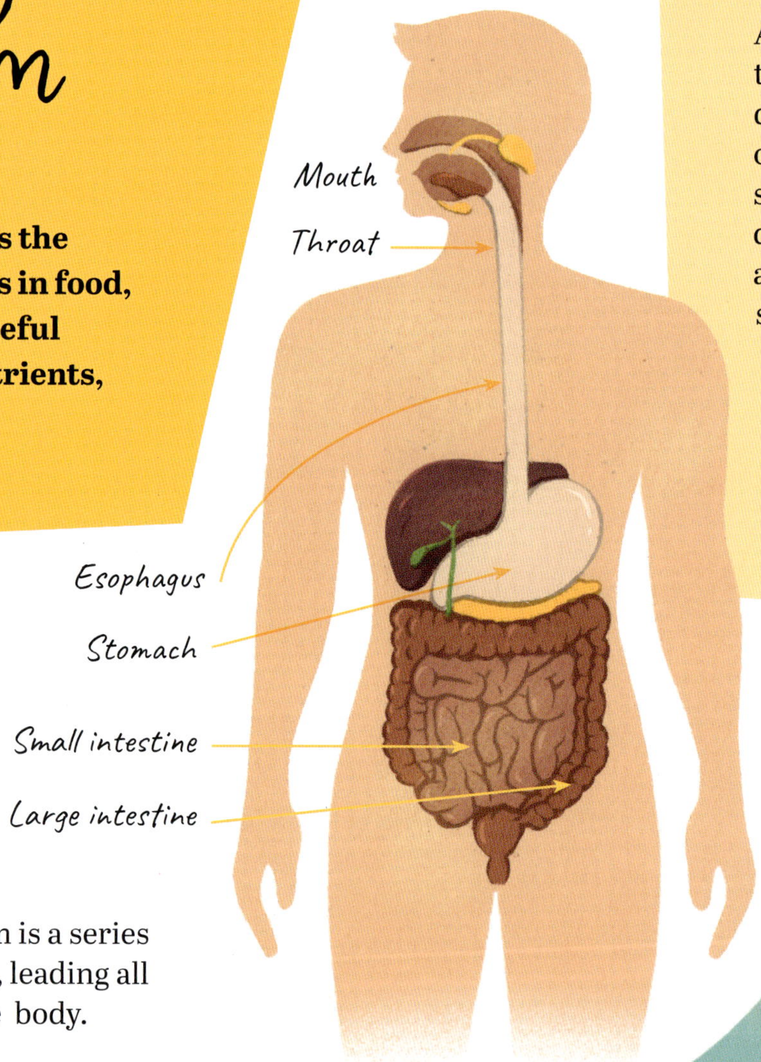

As food passes through, the different parts of the digestive system break it down into smaller and smaller bits, soak up the food chemicals, and collect waste.

The digestive system is a series of tubes and organs, leading all the way through the body.

Chewing and swallowing

The digestive system begins with the mouth. It bites food into pieces, chews them up, and swallows them.

Humans are naturally omnivores, or "everything eaters." Like other animals, our teeth are suited to the types of food we have evolved to eat.

ANIMAL TEETH: PAGE 27

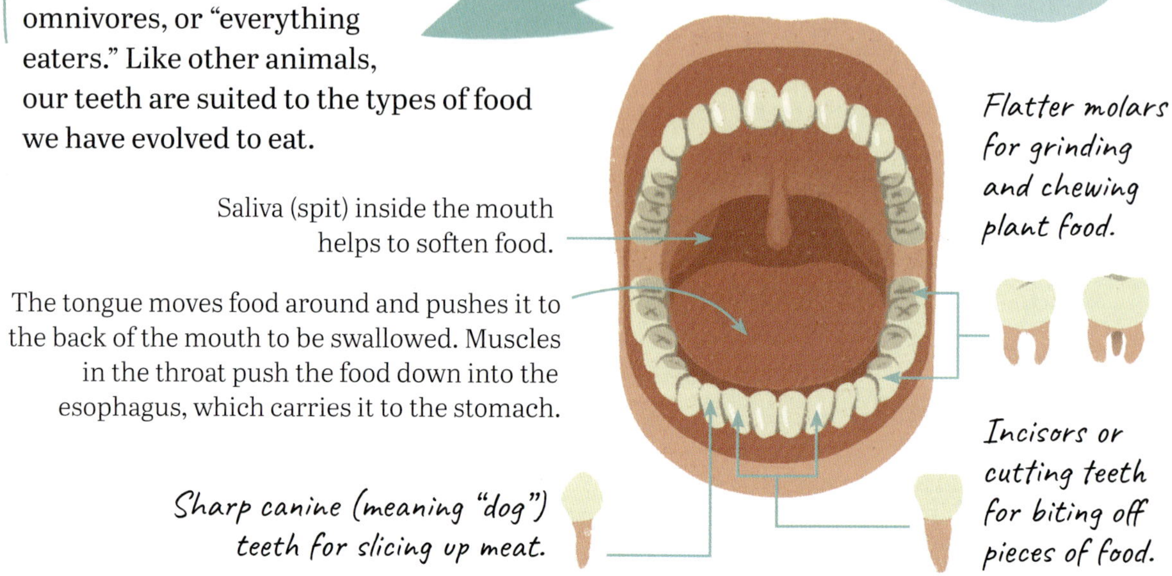

Sitting in the stomach

At the bottom of the esophagus, food squeezes through an opening into the stomach.

An empty stomach is about the size of your fist, but it can stretch to hold lots of food.

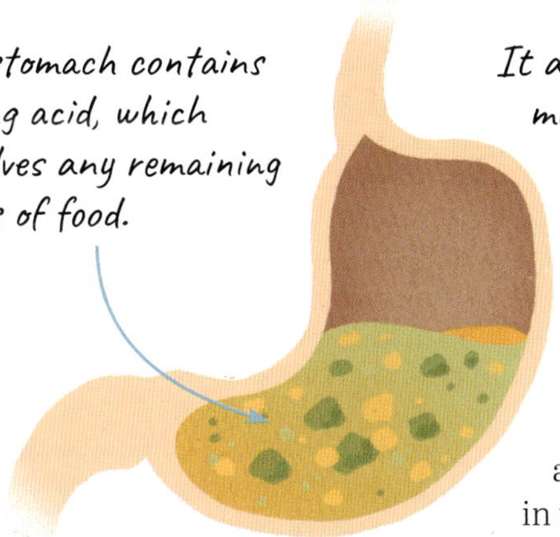

Food spends about four hours in the stomach.

In the intestines

From the stomach, the liquid food squirts into long tubes called the intestines, or guts.

BLOOD: PAGE 43

The small intestine comes first. It's narrow, but very long—more than three times the length of your whole body!

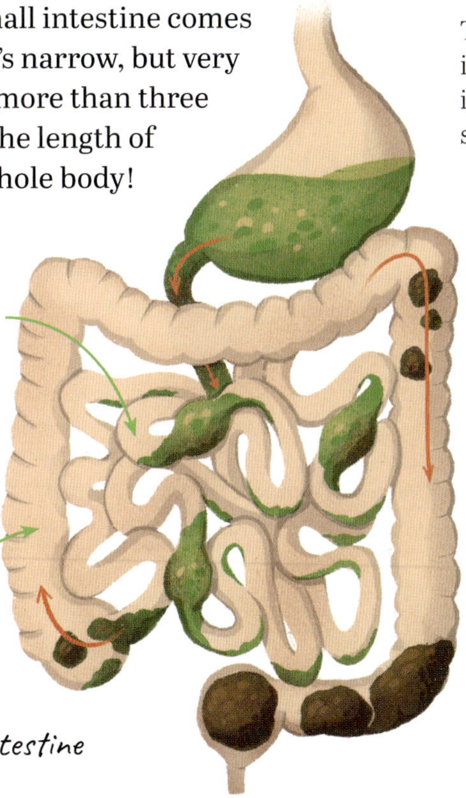

The lining of the small intestine is covered in microscopic finger shapes called villi.

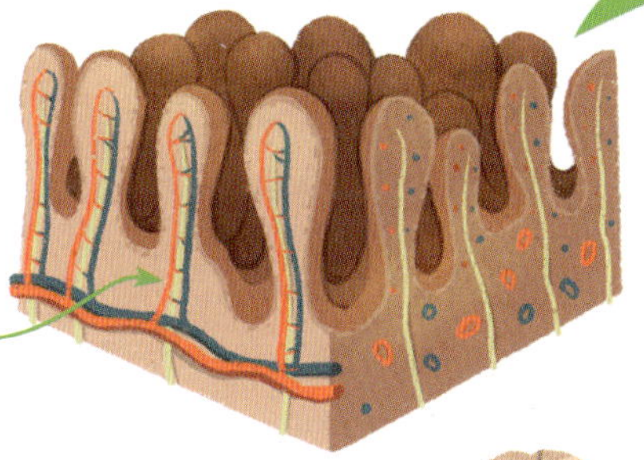

What's left then passes into the large intestine. There, bacteria help to break the last bits of food down to extract useful nutrients.

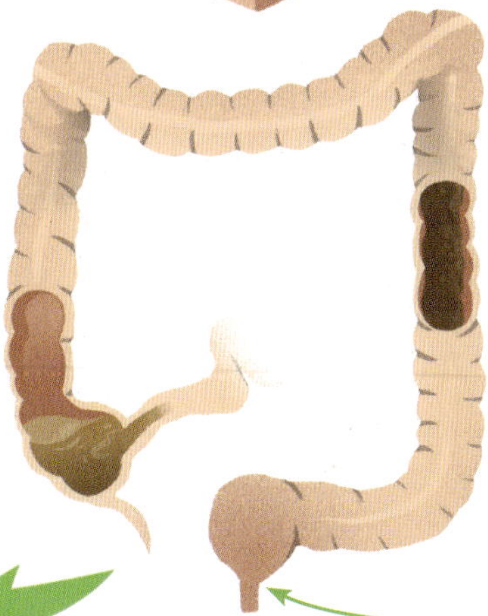

The large intestine also removes water, leaving lumps of waste, or poop!

BACTERIA: PAGE 70

Urinary system

A separate system removes waste water.

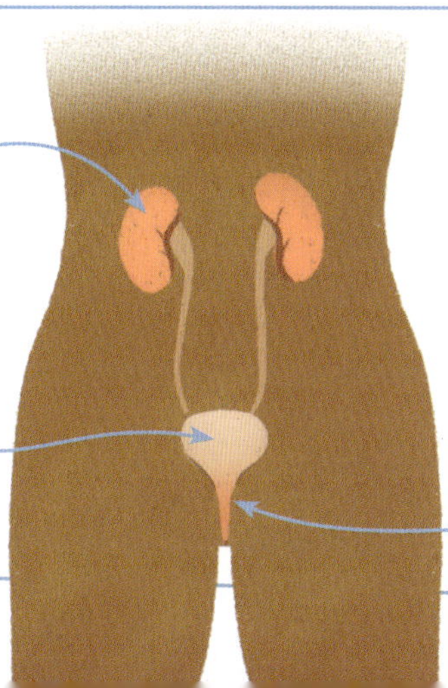

BLOOD: PAGE 43

Heart, lungs, and blood

Two body systems, the respiratory system, and the circulatory system, work together to collect oxygen gas from the air and deliver it around the body.

Body cells need oxygen to turn food into energy so that they can work.

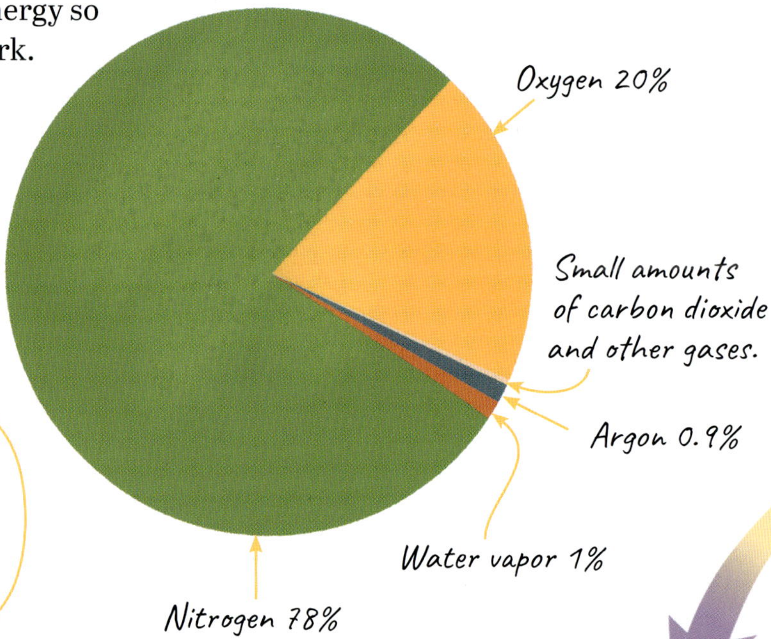

Air is made up of a mixture of gases. About 20 percent of it is oxygen.

Several important organs and body parts help to get the oxygen out of the air and to the body's billions of cells.

CELLS: PAGE 10

Breathing in

We breathe in air using our lungs—two big, spongy organs in the chest.

The lungs expand, or get bigger, when you breathe in, then shrink as they push air out again.

OXYGEN: PAGE 55

Rib muscles, and the diaphragm muscle under the ribs, pull the lungs outward, making them suck in air.

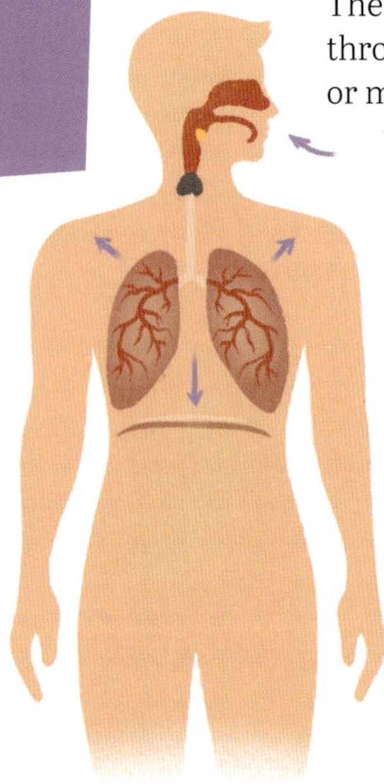

Breathing in

The air flows in through the nose or mouth, down the trachea, or windpipe, and along two branches called the bronchi, filling the lungs.

In the lungs, air flows into millions of tiny pockets called alveoli.

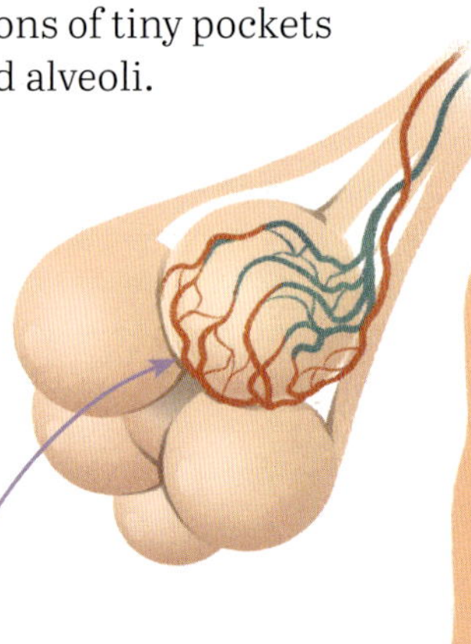

They are surrounded by blood vessels that soak up the oxygen from the air.

At the same time, the blood vessels drop off waste— carbon dioxide gas— from the cells, to be breathed out.

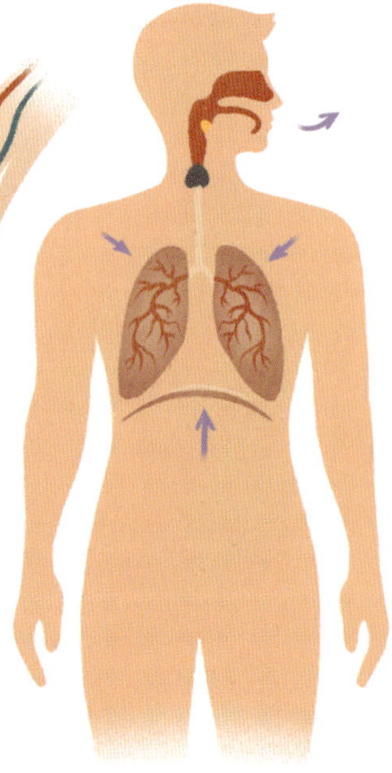

Breathing out

To the heart

Large blood vessels carry the oxygen-filled blood to the heart. The heart's job is to pump the blood around the body to all the cells.

The heart is made of muscle, and works by squeezing. With each squeeze, it pushes some more blood into the blood vessels to be delivered around the body.

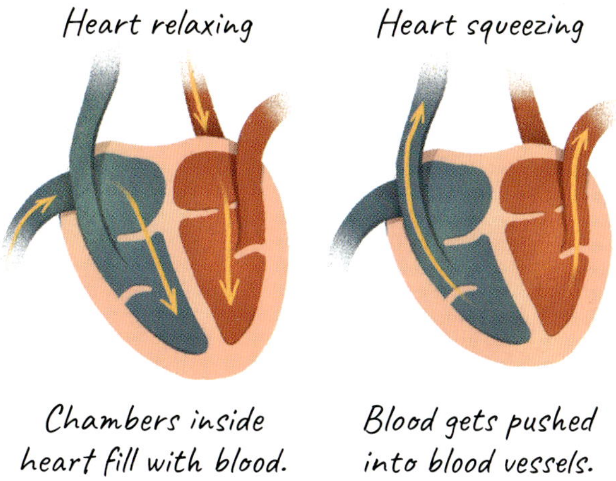

MUSCLES: PAGE 38

HUMAN BRAIN: PAGE 46

Blood's journey

Blood vessels are tubes that carry blood all over the body. Close to the heart, they can be up to 2 cm (0.8 in) across. As they spread out around the body, they get smaller and smaller.

In diagrams, blood vessels are shown in red and blue.

Arteries, shown in red, carry blood away from the heart and deliver it to the cells.

Then the blood flows back along the veins, shown in blue, to collect more oxygen from the lungs.

Blood vessels reach into all the body's tissues and organs, such as skin, muscles, and brain.

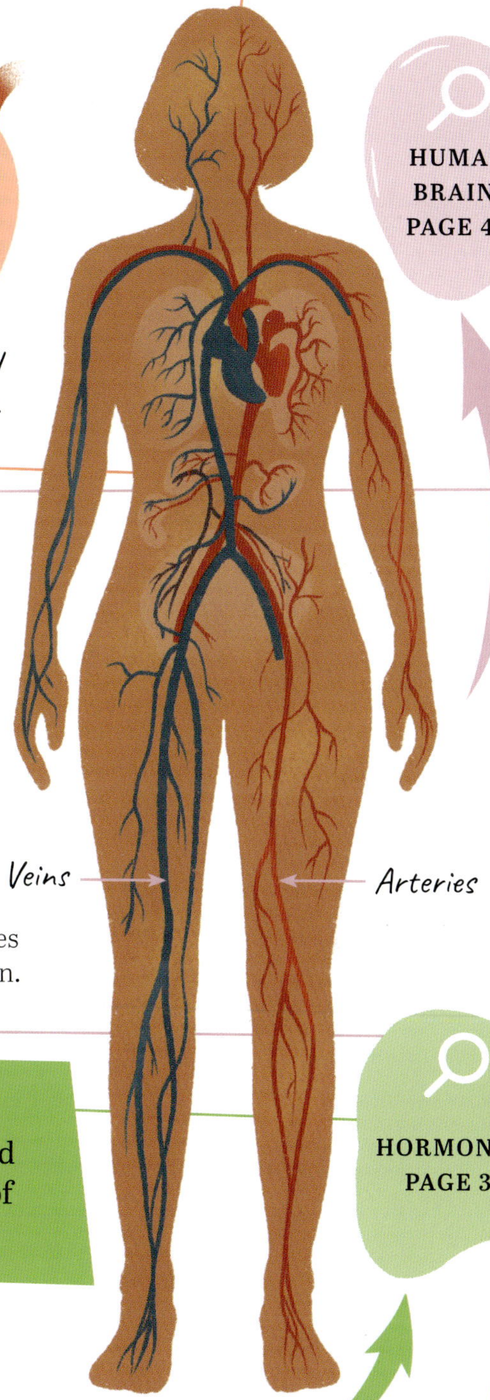

In the blood

Blood is a mixture of a watery liquid called plasma and different types of blood cells.

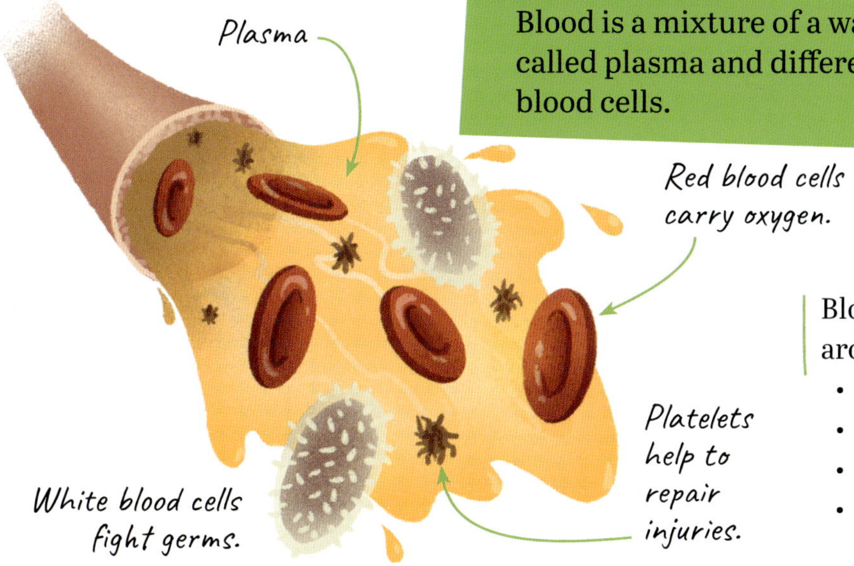

Blood carries other useful things around the body too, including:

- Nutrients, or food chemicals
- Water
- Hormones
- Medicines

HORMONES: PAGE 37

MEDICINE: PAGE 50

Skin, hair, and nails

When you trim your hair or nails, it doesn't hurt, because the cells are no longer alive. The outer layer of your skin is also made of dead cells.

Skin, hair, and nails protect you in various ways, and have other important jobs too.

All these body parts keep growing and growing, to replace the old, dead parts that fall or get trimmed off.

Skin

Skin covers most of your body, protecting and cushioning your insides.

HUMAN SENSES: PAGE 47

Skin cells grow below the surface, then move outward. The top layer of cells are flattened and dead, and eventually flake off. In fact, 40 million of them fall off every day!

Skin has other parts too ...

Different touch-detecting cells feel different sensations:

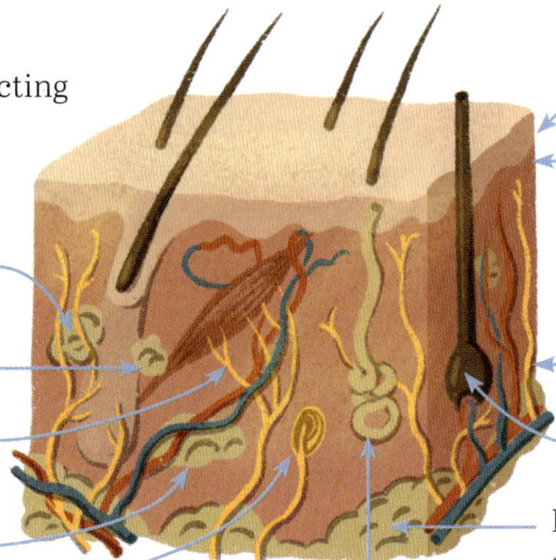

Hair

A human has about **100,000** head hairs, and 5 million hairs all over their body!

MUSCLES: PAGE 38

Each hair grows from a hair follicle in the skin.

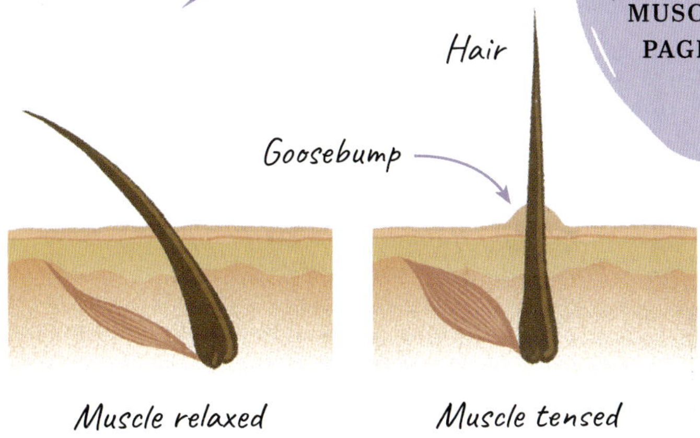

The tiny hairs on your body cause goosebumps! When you're cold, a mini muscle next to each hair pulls it upright, making a bump on the skin. This traps more air next to your skin, helping you warm up.

Nails

Fingernails and toenails grow around 30 mm (1.2 in) per year. The base of the nail is alive, but the tip is made of dead cells.

ANIMAL LIMBS: PAGE 27

Nails grow from a nail matrix under the skin, like this.

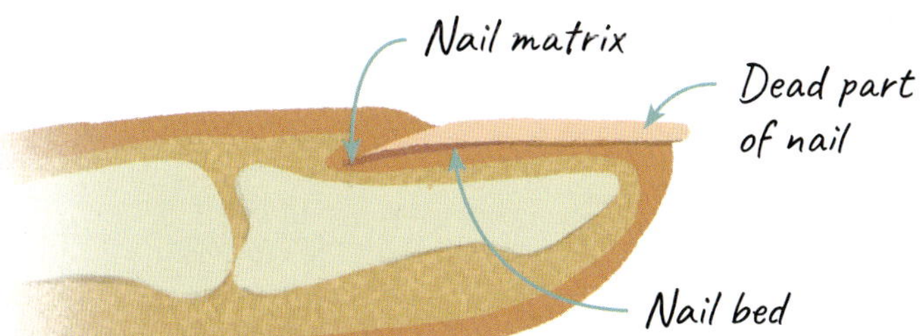

Our nails evolved from animal claws.

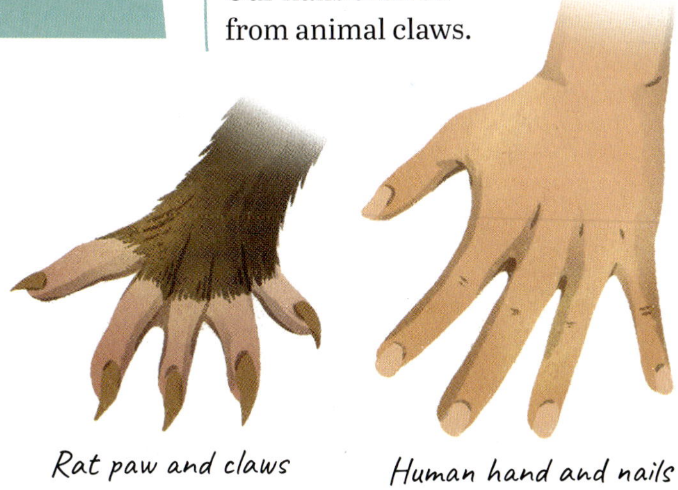

Looking good!

Skin, hair, and nails are important to how we feel and like to look. People all over the world like to decorate, style, and paint them in different ways!

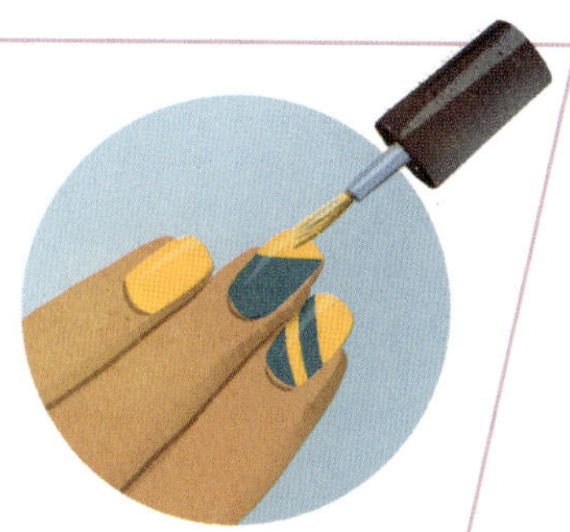

Brain and senses

The brain receives signals from your senses, so that it knows what's going on around you. It also thinks, makes decisions, and sends signals to the body to tell it what to do.

ANIMAL BRAINS AND SENSES: PAGE 30

The brain is linked to the senses, and to the rest of the body, by pathways called nerves.

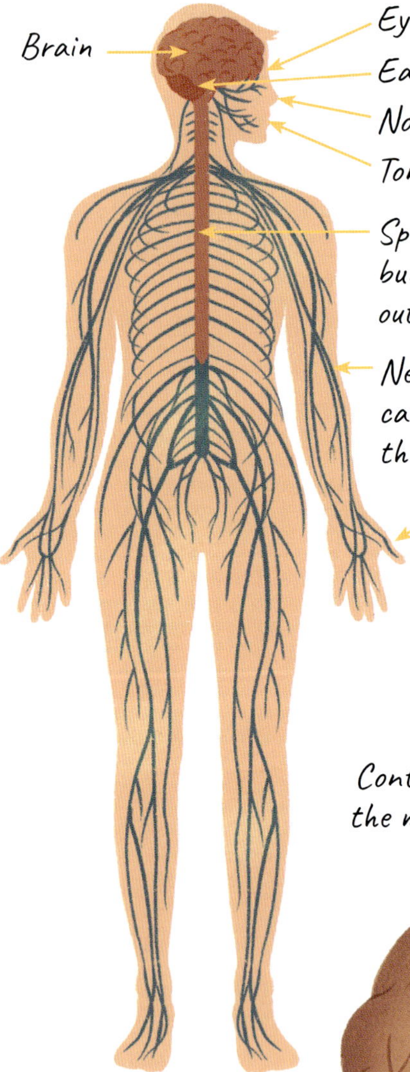

Parts of the brain:

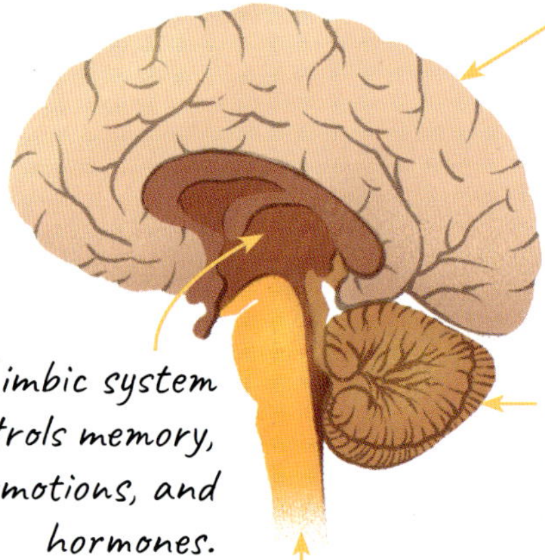

Together, the brain, nerves, and senses make up the nervous system.

The five senses detect your surroundings and send signals to the brain, and the brain sends signals to the muscles and other body parts.

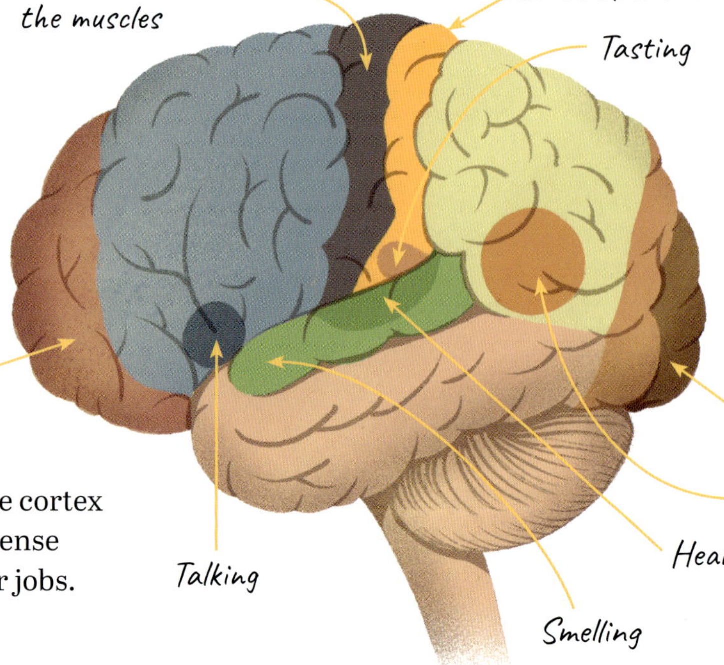

Different parts of the cortex deal with different sense signals, and do other jobs.

Seeing

The eyes are two balls full of clear jelly.

Light shines in through the pupil at the front and hits light-detecting cells on the retina at the back of the eyeball.

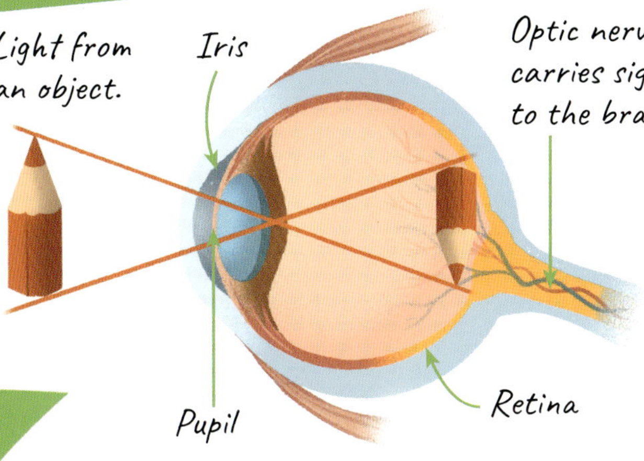

Hearing

Sounds spread out from objects as vibrations, or sound waves, in the air.

The sound waves enter the ears and make them vibrate too.

EAR BONES: PAGE 38

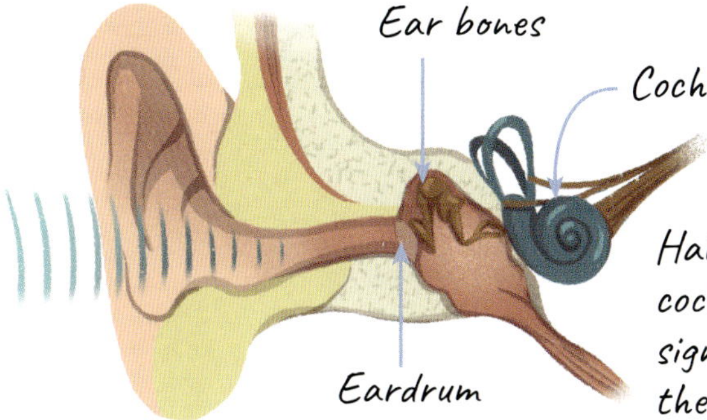

Taste and smell

Taste and smell are closely linked, as the nose helps to detect different tastes.

The mouth and nose are connected by passageways inside the head.

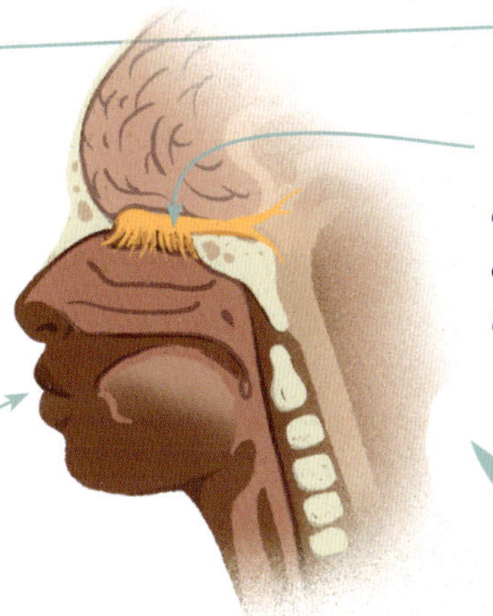

MOUTH: PAGE 40

Sense of touch

There are touch sensors all over the skin and inside the body too.

Nerves reaching all over the body link the touch sensors to the brain.

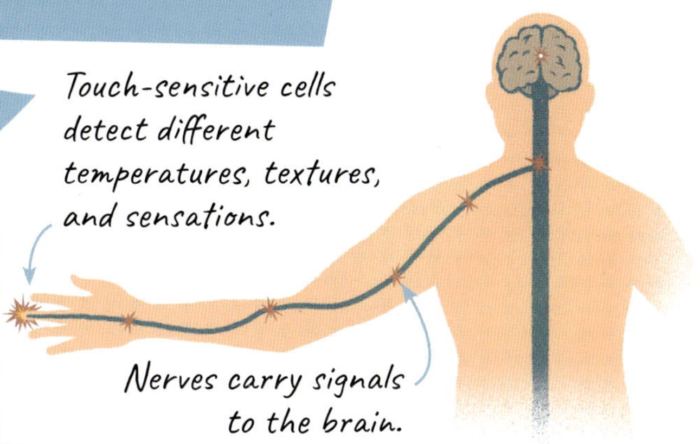

Controlling the body

The brain also sends signals out to different body parts, especially the muscles.

MUSCLES AND BONES: PAGE 38

The signals make muscles move, pulling on the bones and controlling your movements.

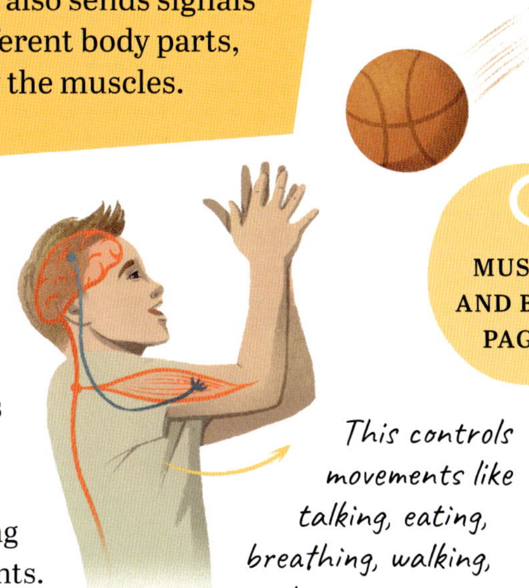

Stages of life

Like other living things, humans go through a life cycle and can reproduce, or have babies.

Compared to most other animals, humans have long lives. It takes us about 18 years to grow up, and we live for an average of 73 years. The oldest person ever lived to be 122!

This diagram shows the human life cycle.

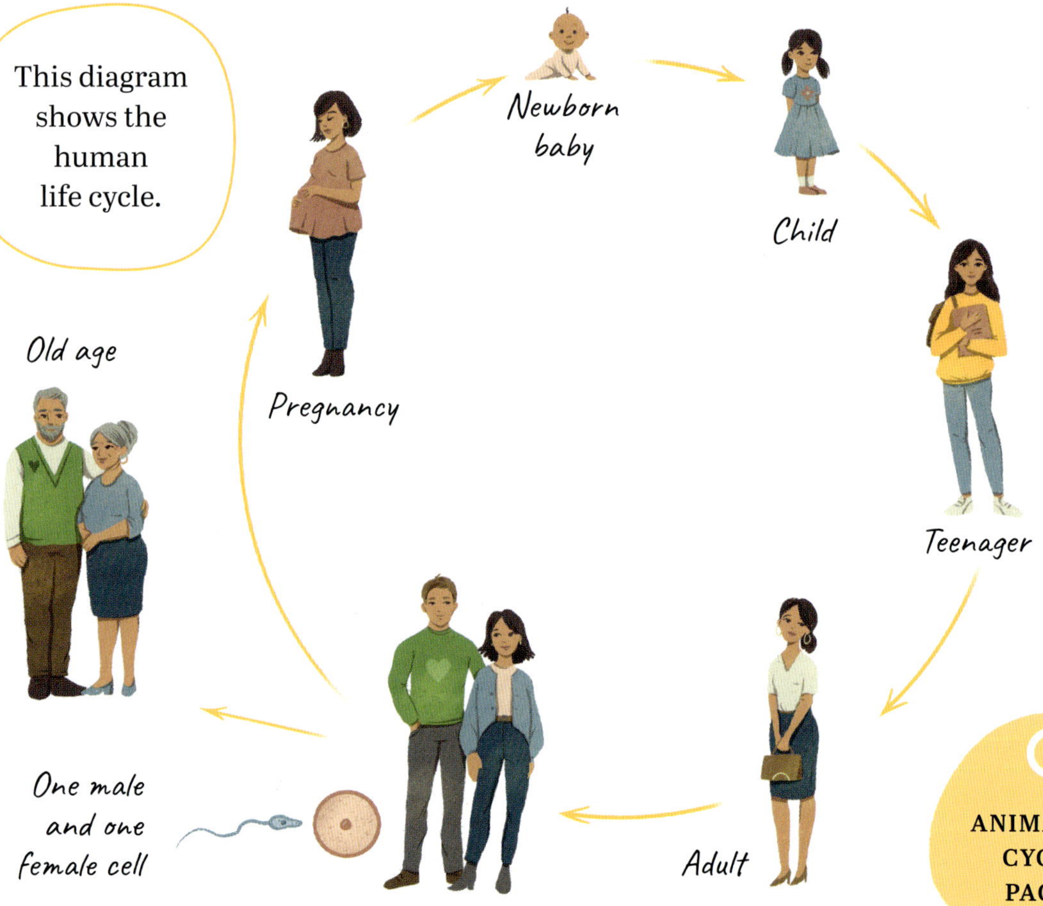

Humans reproduce using sexual reproduction. As in many other animals, the baby grows inside a female's body.

ANIMAL LIFE CYCLES: PAGE 32

Making a baby

To make a baby, a male cell and a female cell have to join together.

When a sperm joins with an egg, the two cells form one new cell, called a zygote. The zygote has the ability to grow into a baby.

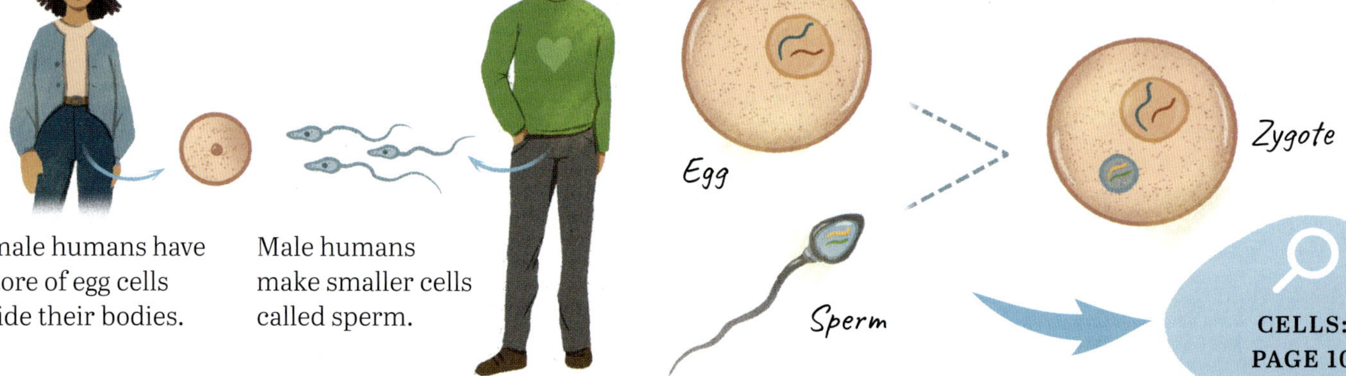

Female humans have a store of egg cells inside their bodies.

Male humans make smaller cells called sperm.

CELLS: PAGE 10

Growing inside

Normally, the two cells join inside a woman's body, and the zygote moves into the womb. This is a very stretchy organ where the baby can grow.

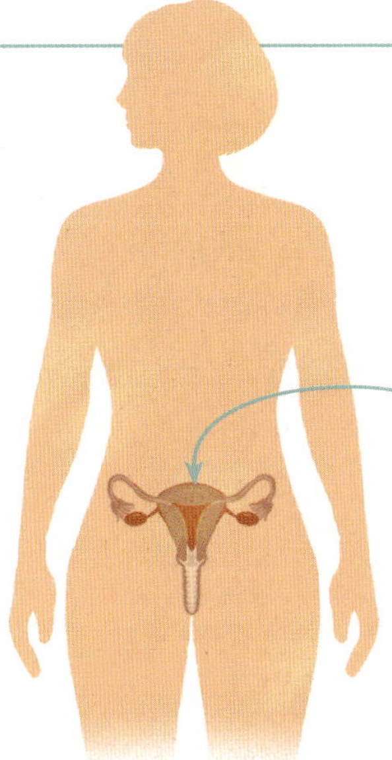

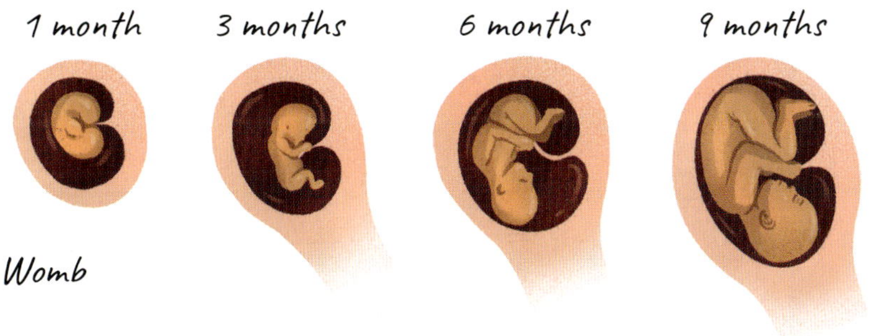

The zygote cell starts to multiply, becoming two cells, then four, then eight, and so on. Over nine months, it keeps growing and forming new body parts, until it's a fully grown baby ready to be born.

Growing and learning

When a baby is born, it is helpless and cannot look after itself, unlike some baby animals. Human parents spend many years caring for their children, feeding them, and teaching them to walk, talk, and look after themselves.

ANIMAL LIFE CYCLES: PAGE 32

MAMMALS: PAGE 23

As humans are mammals, a baby's mother can feed it using milk from her body.

Most children learn to walk at around 1 year old.

And as you get older, you keep learning more things.

Body changes

Our bodies change throughout our lives.

Hair turns grey or white.

People start to shrink slightly.

Skin becomes more wrinkled.

SKIN AND HAIR: PAGE 44

Puberty is the stage when children change into adults. It takes several years, usually sometime between the ages of 10 and 18.

As adults get older and older, more changes happen.

Health and medicine

Being healthy means your body is working well, you feel good, and you can take part in activities. If you do get sick, medicine can often help you get better.

What do we need to stay as healthy as possible? The main things are:

Food

A good balance of foods with all the nutrients we need.

Water

Humans are more than 50% water!

DIGESTION: PAGE 40

Fun and relaxation

Laughing, playing, and relaxing helps you to de-stress and feel good.

Exercise

Moving your body helps to keep it working well.

Sleep

Sleep helps us repair injuries, grow, and store memories.

However, even healthy people can get illnesses and injuries. How do they happen, and how can we fix them?

Germs and diseases

Germs are tiny living things that can invade other living things and make them sick. Our bodies have an immune system that keeps out most germs, but sometimes they get in.

The two main types of germs are bacteria and viruses.

Bacteria are tiny single-celled microorganisms.

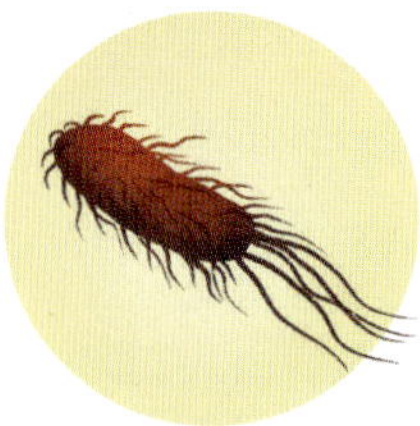

Salmonella food poisoning bacteria

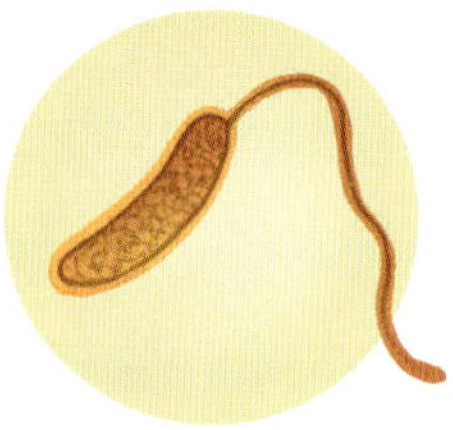

Cholera bacteria

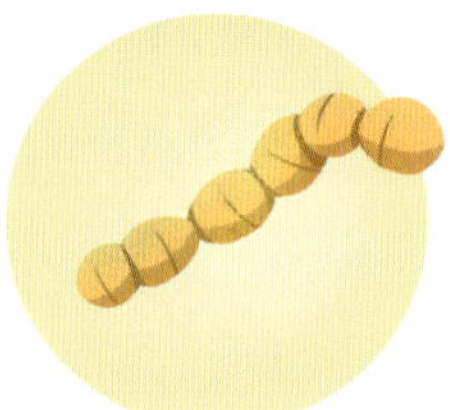

Streptococcus can give you a sore throat.

BACTERIA: PAGE 72

Viruses are even smaller and work by invading living cells.

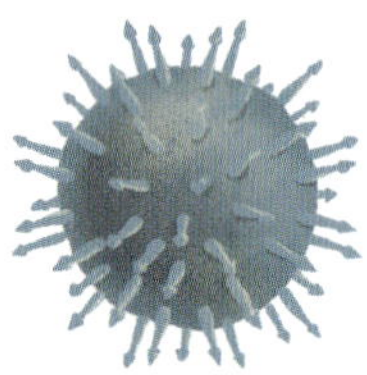

Flu virus

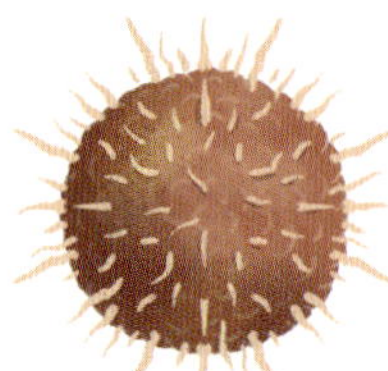

Chickenpox virus

Covid-19 virus

The body can often fight viruses, so you eventually get better.

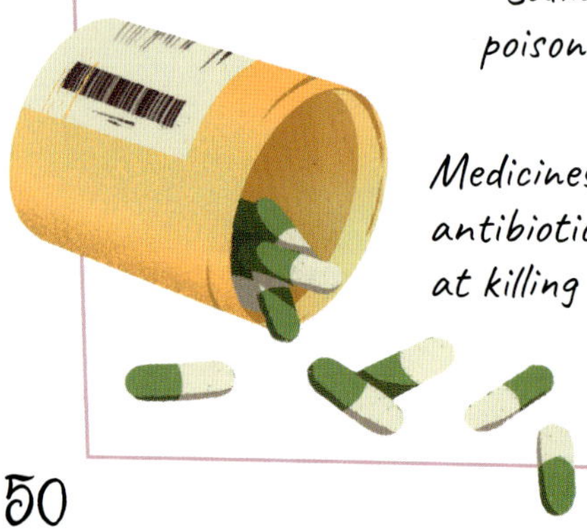

Medicines called antibiotics are good at killing bacteria.

Genes and diseases

Some diseases are caused by differences in a person's genes and DNA, as well as missing genes. These can be passed on from parents to children.

Sickle cell anemia is a genetic disease that makes some red blood cells the wrong shape, so the blood can't carry oxygen very well.

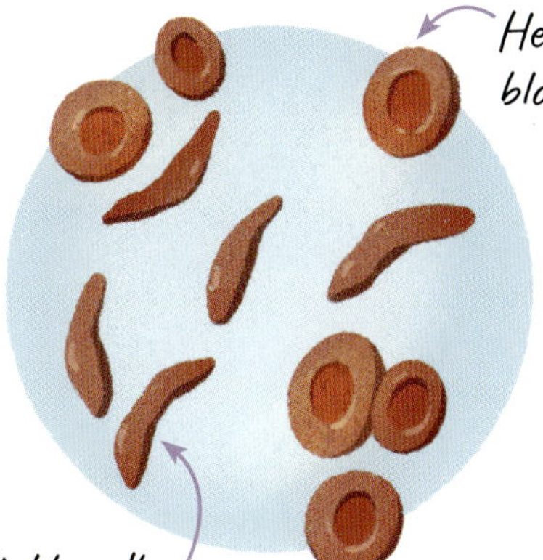

GENES AND DNA: PAGE 12

A blood transfusion can replace the red blood cells, and medicines can help patients to make more healthy cells.

Injuries

The body can get damaged too, but luckily it's quite good at repairing itself.

If you cut your skin, you can lose blood, and germs can get in.

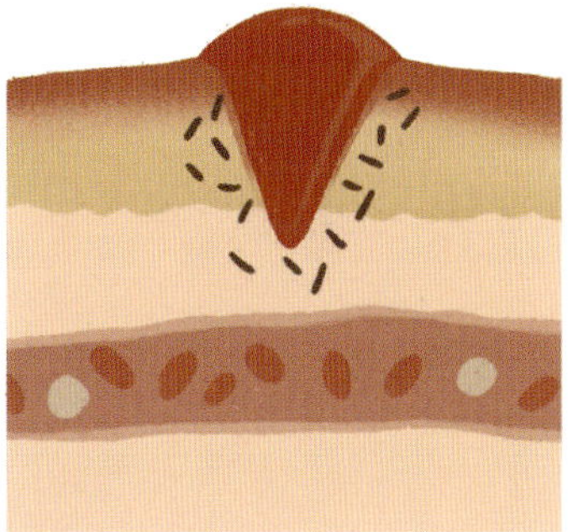

The body sends blood cells to fight germs and block the cut with a blood clot.

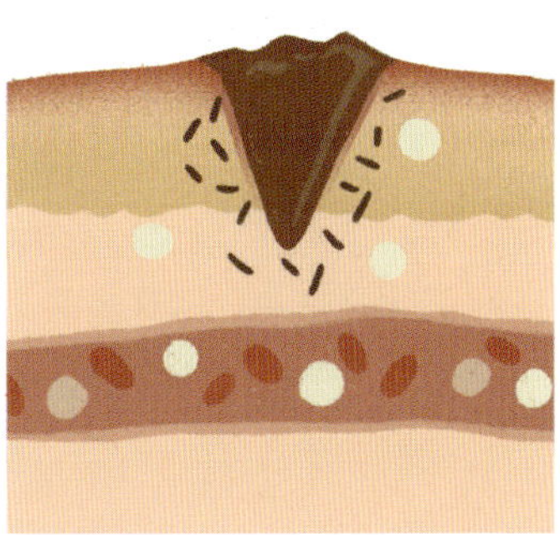

The blood clot hardens into a scab.

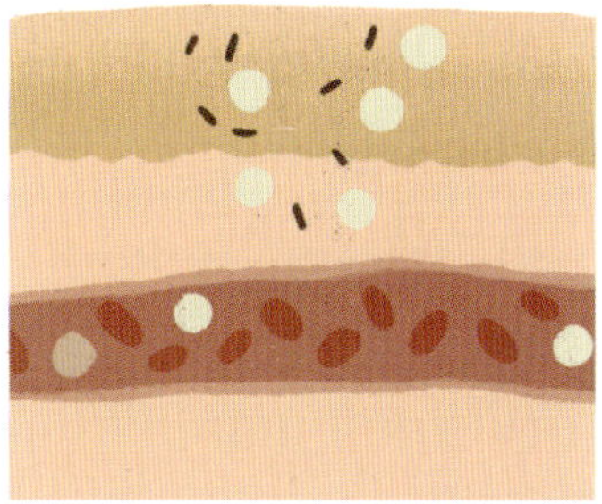

Underneath, the body rebuilds the skin with new cells.

Bones are strong, but they can break, especially arm and leg bones.

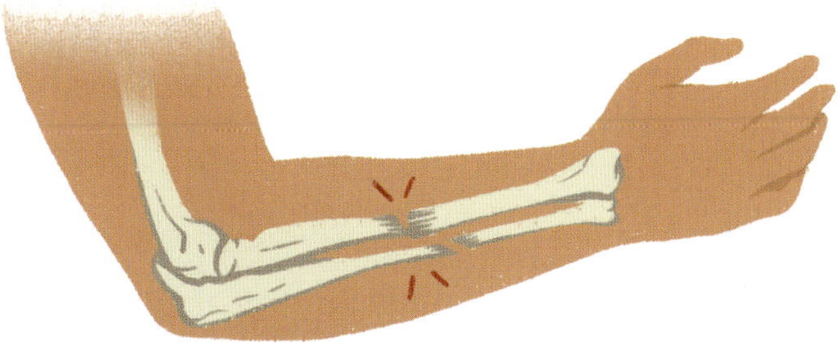

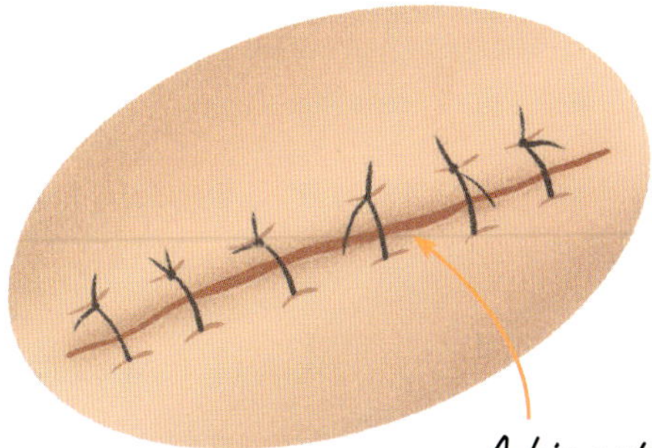

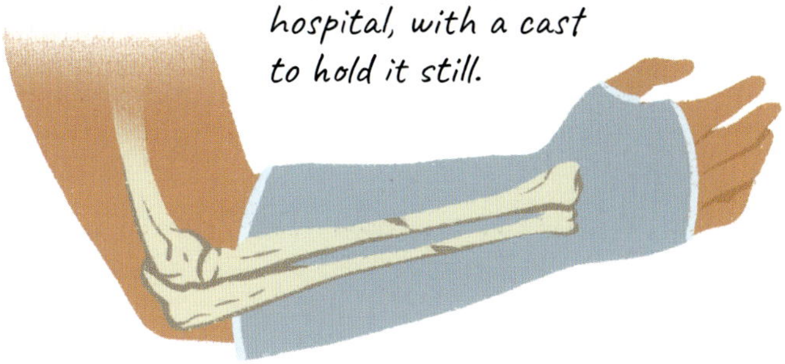

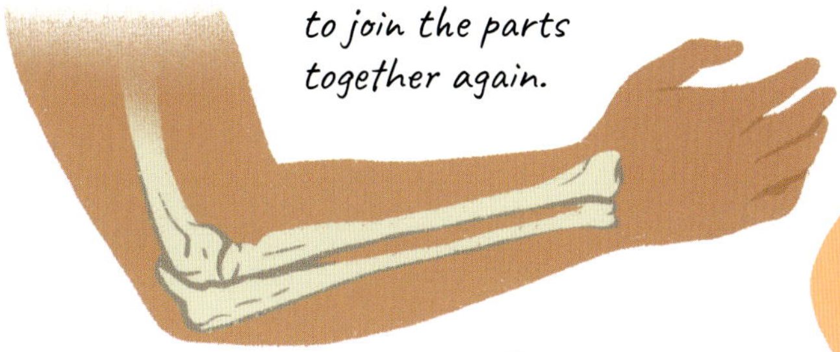

BONES: PAGE 38

What is a plant?

Plants are a very important group of living things. If there weren't any plants, we wouldn't be here!

The study of plants is called botany, and it's an important branch of biology.

This picture shows the main parts of a typical flowering plant. Some plants don't have all these parts, but most well-known plants do.

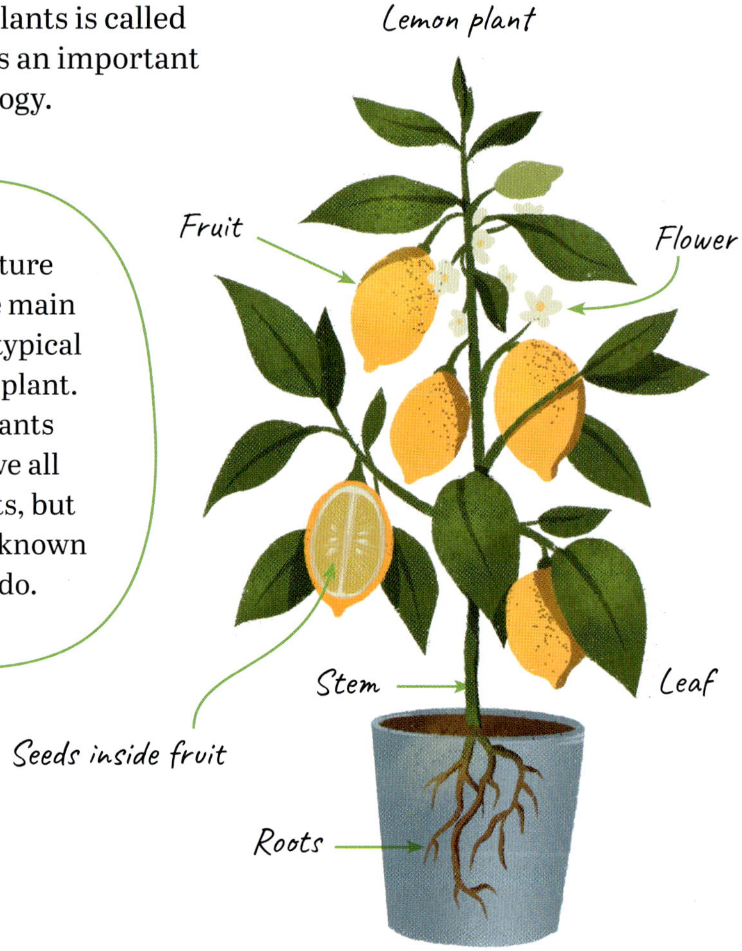

Plants live and feed in a very different way from animals. They don't have mouths and can't eat food like animals can. They also don't need to move around to find food.

Standing still

Like all living things, plants can move, but they don't walk, run, or fly around. Most plants stay in one place, with their roots in the soil.

As well as helping plants to stand up, roots suck up water and nutrients from the soil.

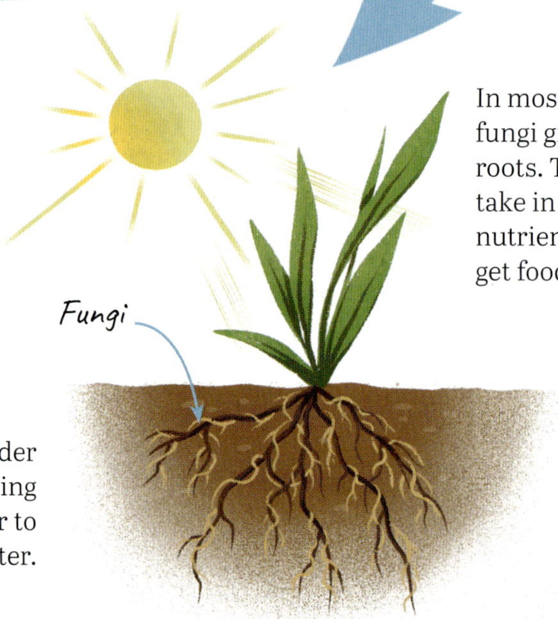

In most plants, a type of fungi grows around the roots. They help the plant take in extra water and nutrients, and in return get food from the plant.

Roots branch out under the soil, becoming smaller and thinner to soak up more water.

FUNGI: PAGE 64

What do plants eat?

Like all living things, plants need food, but they can't get all the food they need from the soil. Instead, they make most of it using sunlight.

Inside the leaves, they use light energy to turn these ingredients into food chemicals.

Plants take in water through their roots ...

... and gas from the air through their leaves.

Plants then use the food to grow and make new plant parts, such as flowers and fruit.

The way plants make food is called photosynthesis.

PHOTOSYNTHESIS: PAGE 54

Travel tubes

In humans and many other animals, blood travels along blood vessels to carry food and water around the body. Plants have a similar system.

Tubes called xylem carry water up from the roots to every part of the plant.

Different tubes called phloem carry food chemicals around the plant.

Xylem carry water.

Phloem carry food.

BLOOD: PAGE 42

Plants and the food chain

Plants use sunlight to grow, providing lots of food for plant-eating animals. They become food for meat-eating animals. So plants are vital to the whole food chain, and most animals depend on them.

In this grassland food chain ...

Wolf hunts deer.

Wolf poop and bones feed bacteria, making soil fertile.

Grass uses soil and sunlight to grow.

Deer feeds on grass.

FOOD CHAINS: PAGE 78

Photosynthesis

Photosynthesis is what happens inside a plant when it uses light energy to make its own food. It means "making with light."

Photosynthesis is a kind of chemical reaction. It starts with two chemicals, which react together and turn into new, different chemicals.

As well as being the way plants get food, photosynthesis plays a big part in keeping the gases in the air balanced—so it helps other living things too.

1. Inside the plant's cells, water combines with carbon dioxide.

2. Light energy, usually from the Sun, makes the reaction start.

3. The chemicals break down and change into glucose, a food chemical, and oxygen. This converts the light energy into chemical energy.

4. The oxygen is released into the air, and the food is sent to other parts of the plant.

Inside the leaves

Photosynthesis mainly happens in a plant's leaves, though it can take place in stems, buds, and other plant parts too.

Plant cells contain organelles (mini organs) called chloroplasts.

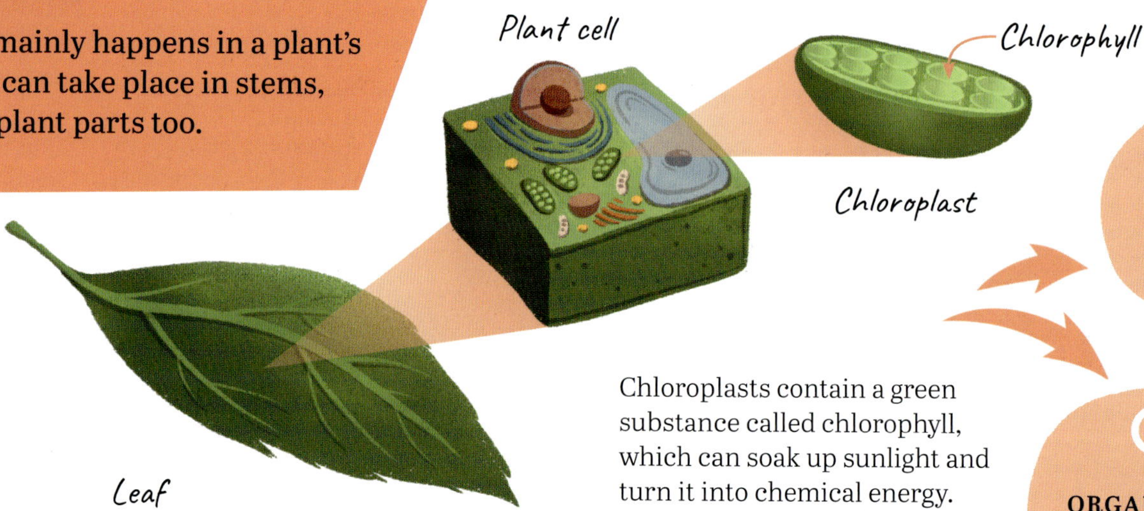

Chloroplasts contain a green substance called chlorophyll, which can soak up sunlight and turn it into chemical energy.

PLANT CELLS: PAGE 11

ORGANELLES: PAGE 10

Releasing oxygen

Carbon dioxide gas is made of carbon and oxygen. Photosynthesis takes the carbon and combines it with the water to make food, leaving the oxygen left over.

OXYGEN: PAGE 42

Leaves have tiny openings in them, called stomata.

Carbon dioxide gas from the air enters leaves through their stomata ...

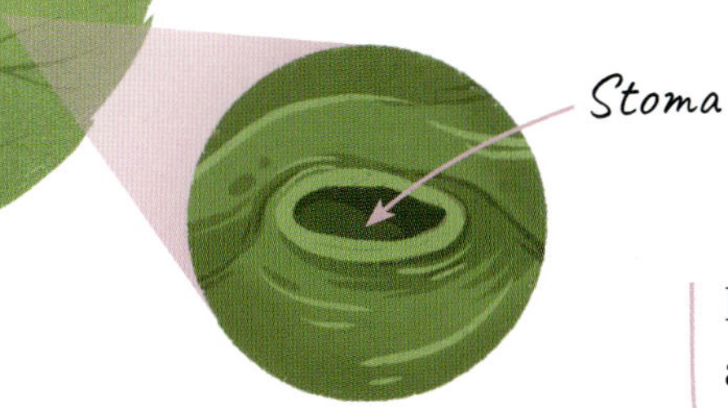

... and the leftover oxygen gas escapes from the stomata too.

Humans and other animals breathe oxygen in, and breathe out carbon dioxide as a waste gas. Plants take in the carbon dioxide and give out oxygen, balancing out the mix of gases in the air.

Capturing carbon

Plants also help to control climate change. Too much carbon dioxide in the air, released by burning fuel, traps heat and causes global warming.

Plants take in carbon dioxide and use it to make food, keeping it out of the air.

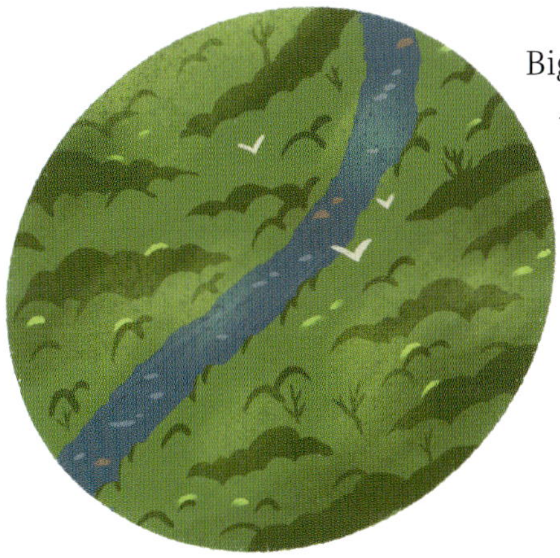

Big forests like the Amazon rainforest take in huge amounts of carbon dioxide and lock away the carbon.

CLIMATE CHANGE: PAGE 84

It's not just plants!

Some other types of living things also use photosynthesis to make food.

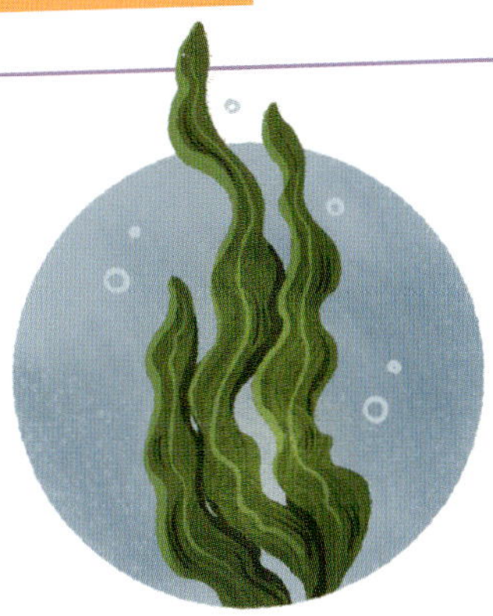

Algae can be single-celled, or bigger. For example, seaweed is a type of algae. It needs light to survive, like plants.

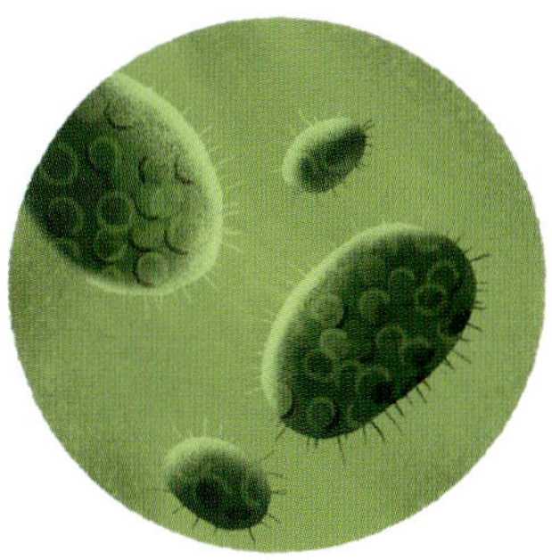

Some bacteria do it too, such as these cyanobacteria.

There are even a few animals that use photosynthesis, such as the leaf sheep—a type of sea slug. It eats algae, and uses the chloroplasts from the algae to do photosynthesis inside its own body.

ALGAE: PAGE 71

BACTERIA: PAGE 70

Types of plants

Botanists have discovered and named about 390,000 different species of plants, from tiny mosses to the tallest trees.

Plants can be sorted, or classified, into several main groups.

This plant family tree shows the main types of plants.

Plant kingdom

- *Plants that have seeds*
  - *Angiosperms, or flowering plants*
    - Flower and fruit trees and bushes
    - Most deciduous trees
    - Wild flowers and garden flowers
    - Grasses
    - Herbs
  - *Gymnosperms, which have seeds but not flowers*
    - *Conifers*
    - *Ginkgos and cycads*
- *Plants that don't have seeds*
  - *Ferns*
  - *Mosses and liverworts*

Plants also come in many different shapes and sizes, and have different adaptations for surviving in different places.

CLASSIFICATION: PAGE 14

Plants with seeds

Plants that make seeds can be angiosperms or gymnosperms.

Strawberry flower

Fruit

Seeds

Cones on a Coulter pine tree

Angiosperms have flowers, which can turn into fruits, nuts, or pods that contain the seeds.

Gymnosperms have cones with seeds inside, or grow fruits without having flowers.

SEEDS: PAGE 59

No seeds!

Most plants do have seeds, but a few do not. Instead, like fungi, they release tiny spores that can grow into new plants.

Seedless plants include ferns, mosses, hornworts, and liverworts.

FUNGI: PAGE 64

Ferns have big, branching leaves.

Bracken or eagle fern

Towering trees

Trees are the biggest plants. You can tell a tree by its thick, strong trunk, made of solid wood with a covering of bark.

However, trees don't all belong to the same plant family. They can be flowering plants, gymnosperms, or even ferns.

The cherry tree, a flowering plant.

Norfolk Island tree fern, a tree in the fern family.

The coast redwood, a conifer, is the tallest tree, growing up to 115 m (377 ft) in height.

FLOWERS: PAGE 58

Water plants

Just like some animals, some plants live in water. Like all plants, water plants need light to survive. So they usually float on or close to the water surface.

Seagrass is the most common type of sea plant. It grows in shallow seas and looks similar to a meadow on land.

Seagrass provides food and shelter for sea creatures, like manatees or sea cows.

Freshwater plants grow in rivers, lakes, streams, and ponds.

Common frogbit grows in still water, such as ponds and canals. Its roots are underwater, but the flowers and leaves float.

Hornwort grows underwater in lakes and streams, and is planted in fish tanks and aquariums.

FISH: PAGE 23

Not a plant

Some things look like plants, but aren't!

Kelp seaweed

Algae, such as seaweed, are not plants, although they are closely related.

Fungi, such as mushrooms, are not plants—they belong to a separate kingdom of living things.

Verdigris agaric mushrooms are greenish, but are not plants.

FUNGI: PAGE 64

Flowers, pollen, and seeds

Flowers contain ingredients for making seeds so that flowering plants can reproduce and make new plants.

Flowers come in many shapes, sizes, and hues, but most have the same main parts.

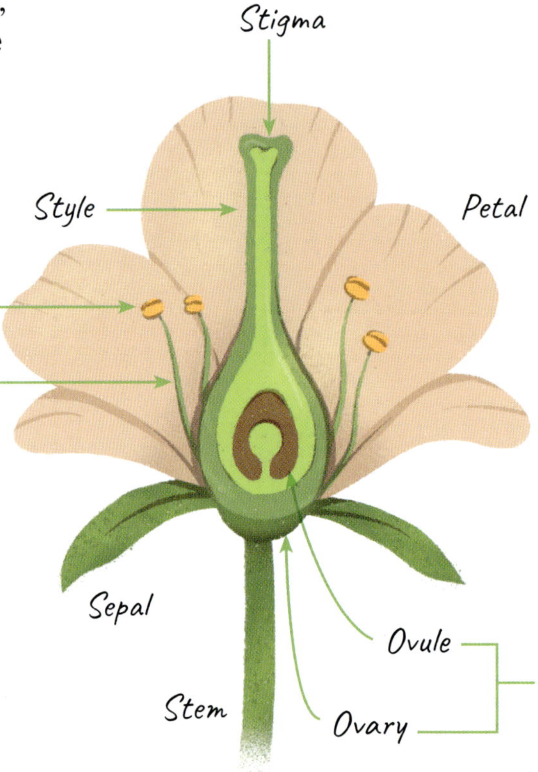

Stamen, or male part of a flower, which makes pollen.

Pistil, or female part of a flower, where seeds can grow.

This flower is shown cut in half so you can see all the parts clearly.

Many flowers have both male and female parts, but some only have one or the other.

Pollination

Pollination happens when pollen from the stamen, or male part of a flower, lands on the stigma, at the top of the pistil, or female part of a flower.

When a pollen grain lands on a stigma, it grows a tube down inside the stigma, and delivers male sperm cells to an ovule.

This fertilizes a female egg cell, which can then become a seed.

CELLS PAGE 10

Pollinators

Some plants, such as grasses, let their pollen blow from one flower to another on the wind. But many others rely on animals, known as pollinators, to pollinate them.

BIRDS: PAGE 23

Bees are common pollinators.

Flowers make a sweet liquid nectar to attract bees and other insects.

As bees feed on the nectar, pollen sticks to them, and brushes off onto the next flower they visit.

Other animals can be pollinators too, including moths, wasps, bats, birds, and lemurs.

The black-ruffed lemur pollinates plants as it moves around eating flowers and fruit.

INSECTS PAGE 24

Fruits and seeds

As the seeds grow, most plants grow a fruit, pod, shell, or other covering around them.

These are all seeds, with different types of coverings, pods, or fruits.

A hazelnut is a seed inside a hard shell.

A cherry is a soft fruit around a hard seed.

Sycamore tree seeds grow inside a wing-shaped case.

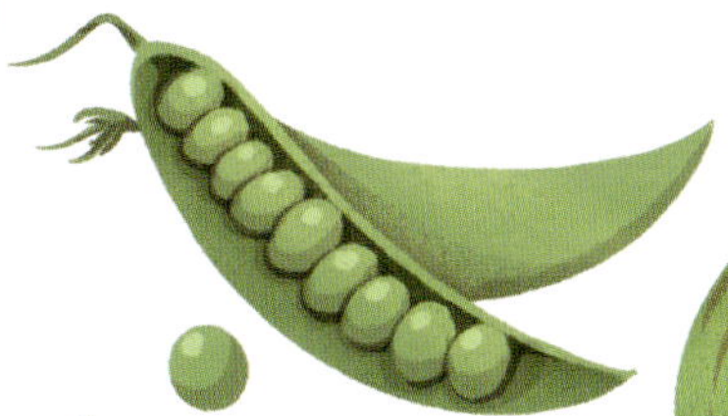

Peas are seeds that grow in a pod.

A coconut is a big seed inside an even bigger fruit.

TREES: PAGE 57

Spreading seeds

Once plants have made their seeds, they need them to disperse, or spread out, over a wide area to find a place to grow.

Seeds have several ways of dispersing:

Dandelion seed

Some have wings or fluffy parachutes that help them fly in the wind.

Some plants can pop or squirt their seeds away from them.

Squirting cucumber

Fruit bats eat lychees and disperse their seeds.

Some have fruits that animals like to eat. Later, the seeds fall out in their droppings.

ANIMAL FOOD: PAGE 28

Life without flowers

Not all plants need flowers to reproduce. Non-flowering plants use other methods.

Non-flowering plants include conifers, ginkgos, cycads, ferns, mosses, and horsetails and their relatives. They can be divided into two main groups.

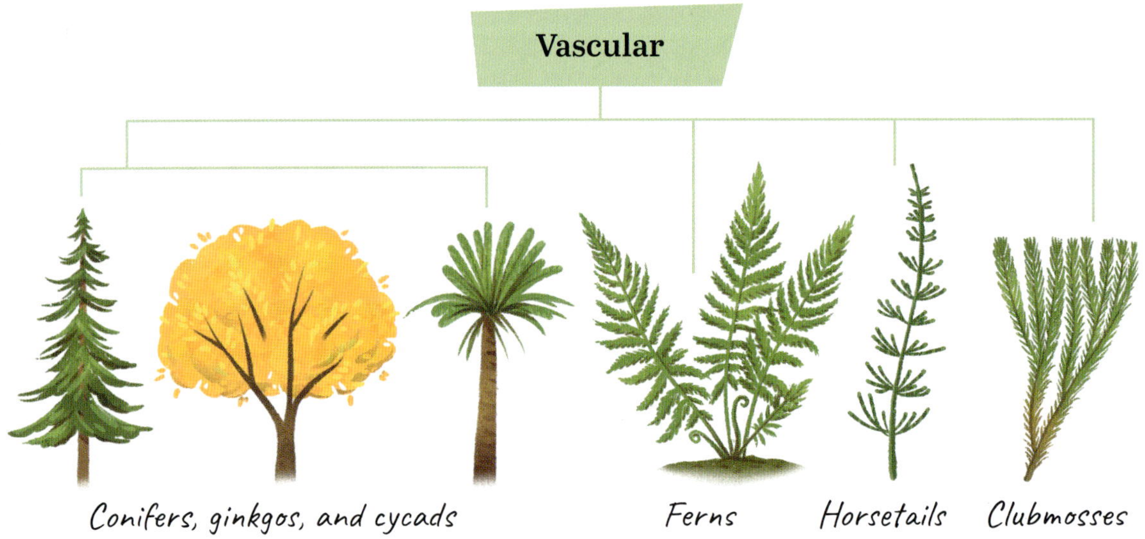

Most of them, like flowering plants, are vascular plants. That means they have xylem and phloem tubes inside them that carry water and food around the plant.

But a few, like mosses, hornworts, and liverworts, are non-vascular plants and don't have these tubes. Instead, water and food chemicals just soak through them. Because of this, they can't grow very big.

Without flowers, how do these plants make new plants? Some can make seeds in other ways, while some use a different method: tiny, dust-like spores.

Cones instead of flowers

Conifers get their name because instead of flowers, they have cones!

Most conifers are trees, but some are bushes. They have thin, needle-shaped leaves, and their seeds grow inside cones.

The cones hold the seeds inside, and open up or fall apart to release the seeds.

TREES: PAGE 57

Ginkgos and cycads

Ginkgos and cycads are unusual trees with a long history. They evolved before flowering plants, and were common in the time of the dinosaurs—some species are still around today.

The ginkgo tree has parts that make fruits and seeds, but no flowers.

Cycads make their seeds in big cones.

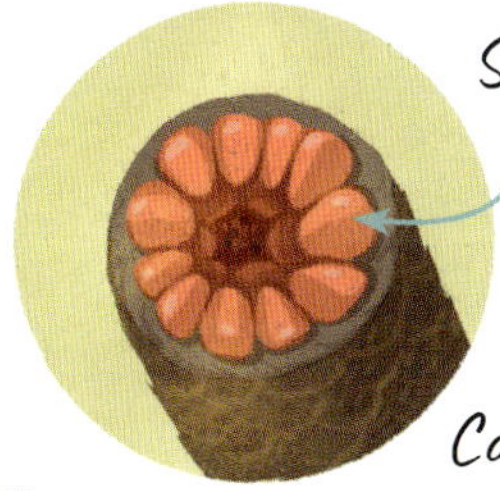

Cycads look similar to palm trees

DINOSAURS: PAGE 19

Ferns, clubmosses, and horsetails

These plants don't have seeds at all. Instead, they have spores. They are cells that can grow into new plants and are so small they look like fine powder.

CELLS: PAGE 10

Ferns release their spores from spots on their leaves called sori.

Mosses, hornworts, and liverworts

These simple plants have no xylem and phloem and no seeds. They grow close to the ground or on walls, trees, or rocks, and release spores to reproduce.

Mosses grow little capsules containing their spores, which open or explode to release them into the air.

SPORES: PAGE 65

Useful plants

We rely on plants for all kinds of everyday things. Imagine life without all the plants on these pages!

We grow thousands of different plant crops all over the world, mainly to use as food, but for many other purposes too.

The world's biggest crop is sugarcane, a type of giant grass plant.

The sugar is extracted from the plant's stems.

STEMS:
PAGE 52

As well as farming them as crops, we use some plants that can be collected from the wild.

Woven nettle fabric

Stinging nettles are usually seen as a weed, but they can be made into soup, tea, or fabric.

We use plants in so many different ways, you might not realize how many things come from them.

Plant food

Even if you're not a vegetarian, you almost certainly still eat lots of plants.

Besides fresh fruit and vegetables, other foods like bread, breakfast cereal, pasta, chips, cooking oil, chocolate, coffee, and tea all come from plants.

Bread and pasta are both made from wheat.

Coffee bush with coffee berries

FOOD:
PAGE 28

Plant fabrics

A lot of our clothes are made from plants too, especially cotton.

Cotton plant

Cotton plants grow white fluff around their seeds. This fluff can be spun into thread and used to make fabric.

Fluffy cotton "ball"

We also make fabrics from:

- Flax plants, used to make linen
- Kapok
- Ramie, a relative of nettles
- Hemp
- Bamboo
- Pineapple leaves

SEEDS: PAGE 59

Building and making

Look around and you'll almost certainly see something made of wood. This natural material forms inside trees and bushes to give them strength and hold them up.

Bamboo, another giant grass, can be used like wood.

We use wood to make buildings, boats, furniture, and all kinds of everyday objects.

Shed

Bamboo chair

Desk

Wooden toys

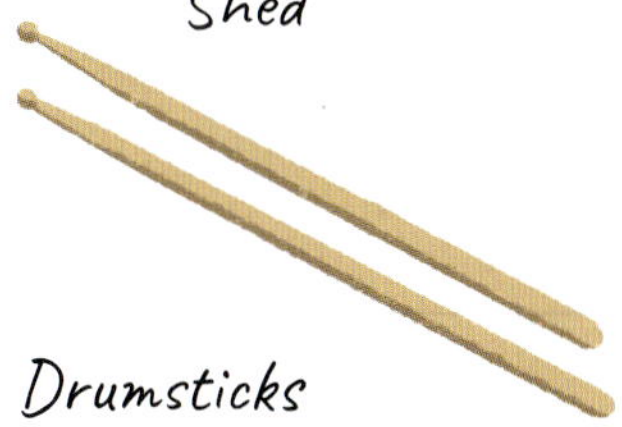

Drumsticks

TREES: PAGE 57

Fabulous flowers

Plants make beautiful, vibrant, scented flowers to attract the insects or other animals that pollinate them. But we humans love them too!

Flower farmers grow flowers to sell as gifts and decorations, as garden plants, and to make perfumes, soap, tea, dyes, and medicines.

POLLINATION: PAGE 58

Tulip flowers growing in the Netherlands.

What are fungi?

Fungi are not plants, but a completely different kingdom of living things. They seem similar to plants, as they stay in one place. However, fungi don't make food using sunlight like plants do. Instead they soak up food from their surroundings.

Scientists have discovered almost 150,000 different species of fungi. They include tiny single-celled fungi and bigger multi-celled fungi, like mushrooms.

PLANT AND ANIMAL CELLS: PAGE 11

Mushrooms are the most familiar fungi, but they have an underground part that you rarely see.

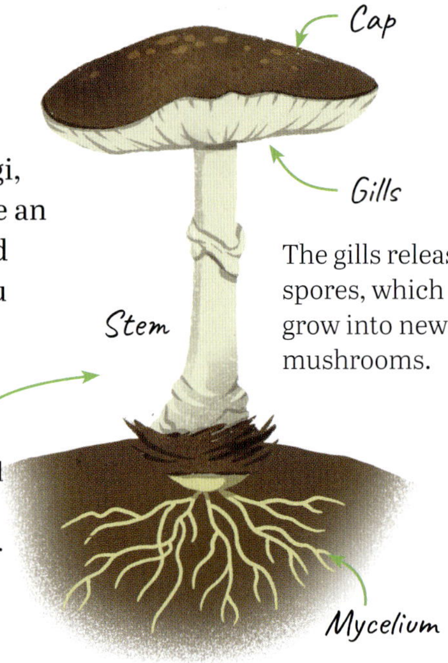

The gills release spores, which can grow into new mushrooms.

The part above ground is called the fruiting body.

The mycelium is a network of thread-like roots, or hyphae. They reach into the soil, or into other food sources, such as a rotting log, to collect food chemicals.

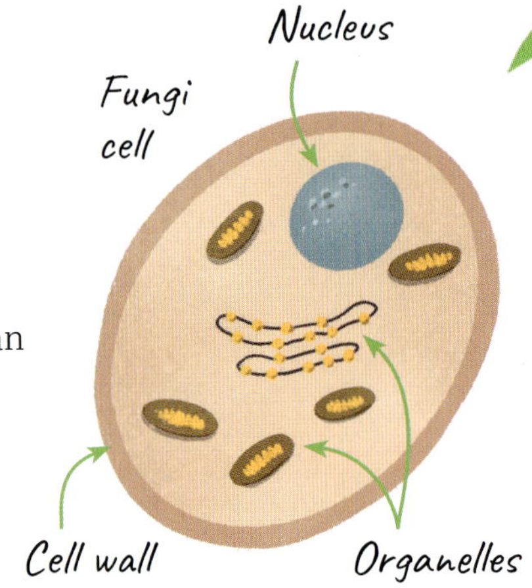

Fungi cells are different from plant and animal cells. Like plant cells, they have a strong cell wall, but it's usually made of a different material, called chitin.

The different types of fungi live in a wide range of places: soil, water, on walls and rocks, and on other living things (including humans!)

Mushrooms and toadstools

Mushrooms and toadstools are multi-celled fungi with a fruiting body that can grow very quickly.

Mushrooms and toadstools all belong to the same group. The word "mushroom" is sometimes used to mean the species we can eat, while "toadstools" is used for poisonous types.

It can be hard to tell the difference between poisonous and edible fungi, which is why you should never pick and eat them from the wild without expert advice.

FOOD: PAGE 28

Molds

Molds are similar to mushrooms and toadstools, but smaller. They often grow on old food, such as bread, cheese, or fruit.

The mold grows hyphae that reach into the food, making it rot and decay, or decompose.

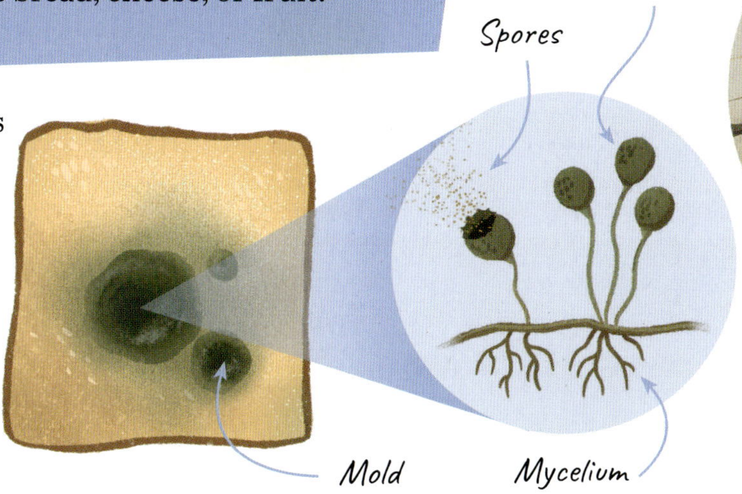

Molds can grow in other places too, like on old books or in damp walls.

DECOMPOSING: PAGE 81

Yeasts

Yeasts are much smaller, simpler fungi that have only one cell each and are a type of microorganism.

Instead of growing and releasing spores, yeast cells reproduce by budding.

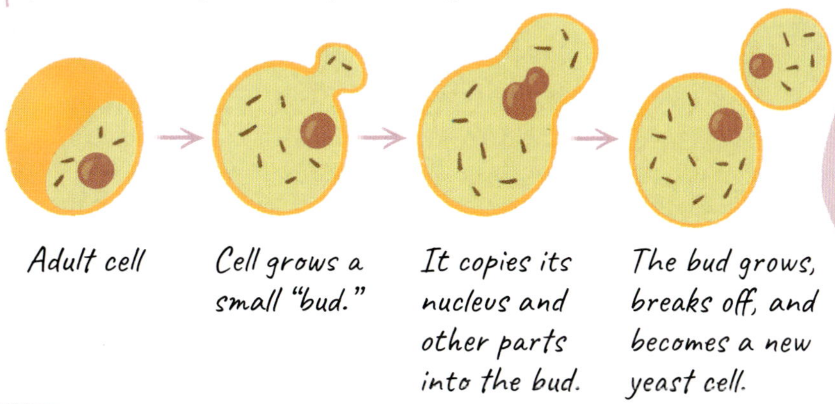

MICROORGANISMS: PAGE 70

Lichens

Lichens are flat, flaky life forms that grow on rocks and walls. They are made of fungi and algae living together and helping each other.

The fungus protects the algae that live inside it.

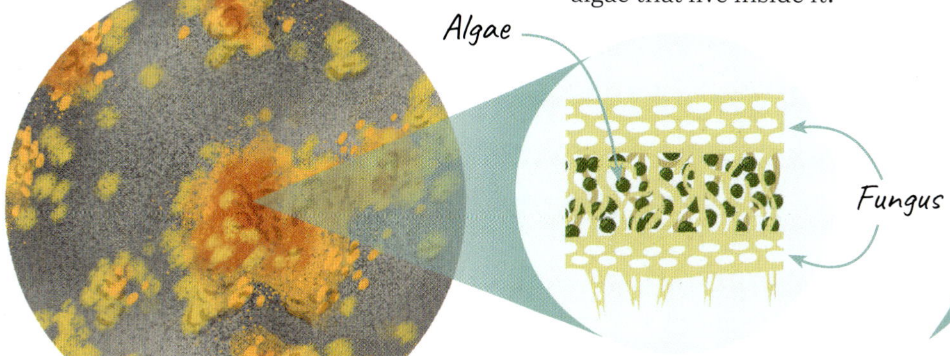

The algae use sunlight to make food and share it with the fungus.

ALGAE: PAGE 71

Useful and harmful fungi

Like plants and animals, fungi can be very useful to us.

We use some types of fungi as food, while others are used in making food and other useful things.

Fungi can often grow very quickly, and some release gases and other chemicals as they feed. That can be good or bad for us, depending on the type of fungi.

Mushrooms are used like a type of vegetable, even though they are not plants.

But some fungi can be very dangerous, such as poisonous toadstools.

Eating just half of one death cap toadstool can be deadly.

Fungus food

Many types of mushrooms are used in cooking, but that's not the only way we use fungi in food.

Some molds are edible and are used in certain types of cheese.

The blue streaks are a type of tasty mold.

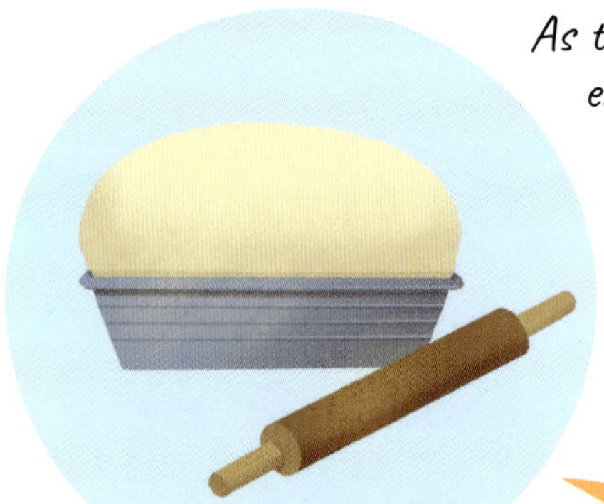

As the yeast feeds and excretes (or releases) gas, the dough gets filled with bubbles, making it soft and chewy when it's cooked.

Baker's yeast is added to bread dough. The yeast cells release gas that makes the dough rise.

EXCRETION: PAGE 7

Making medicines

Molds can be attacked by harmful bacteria, so some make germ-killing chemicals called antibiotics to defend themselves.

We use several types of mold to make antibiotic medicines.

Antibiotics have saved millions of lives by killing germs that cause dangerous diseases, such as TB (tuberculosis), cholera, and whooping cough.

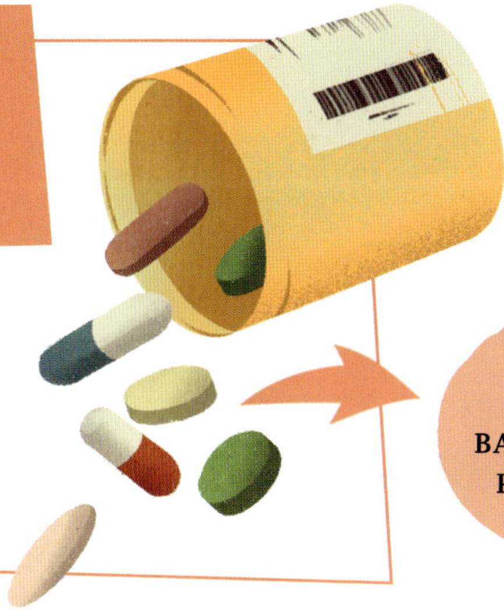

BACTERIA: PAGE 70

Germs and diseases

Sometimes, though, fungi themselves can be germs and cause diseases.

Fungi known as smuts, scabs, and rusts can infect and damage plants. They cause big problems for crop farmers.

An apple damaged by apple scab fungus.

Some disease fungi can affect humans, too.

Ringworm is a skin disease caused by a fungus. It causes an itchy ring-shaped rash.

GERMS AND DISEASES: PAGE 72

CROPS PAGE 62

Toxic fungi

Besides toadstools, some other kinds of fungi can poison people.

Some types of mold spores are harmful if you breathe them in. They can cause lung diseases or make people's asthma worse.

Barley infected with ergot fungus.

When fungus called ergot grows on grains like wheat and barley, it can poison them and make people sick.

LUNGS: PAGE 42

What is microbiology?

Microbiology is the study of tiny living things—so tiny, you need a microscope to see them! They are known as microorganisms, or microbes.

CELLS: PAGE 10

There are many different species and types of microorganisms, but they are all single-celled, meaning they have only one cell each. They include bacteria, archaea, single-celled algae, single-celled fungi, and protists.

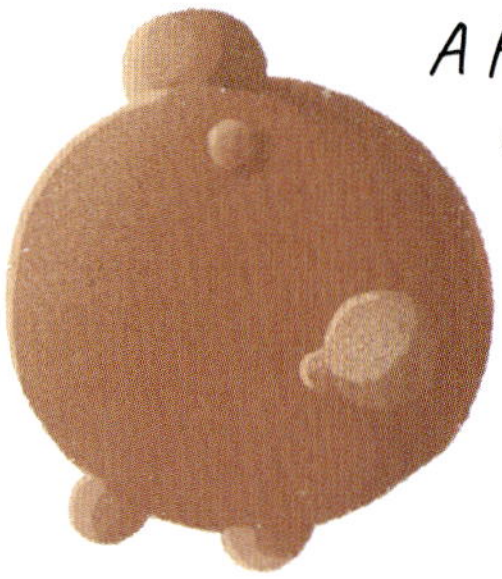

A Haloferax archaeon, which lives in salty water.

Tuberculosis bacteria

A diatom, a type of single-celled algae.

An amoeba, a type of protist.

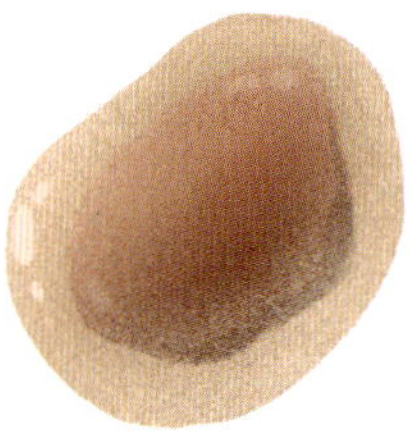

A single-celled fungus found in soil.

Microorganisms are a very important part of biology. They live almost everywhere and have a big impact on other living things.

Working with microscopes

To study microorganisms, scientists need microscopes. They make microorganisms look bigger, so you can get a good look at them.

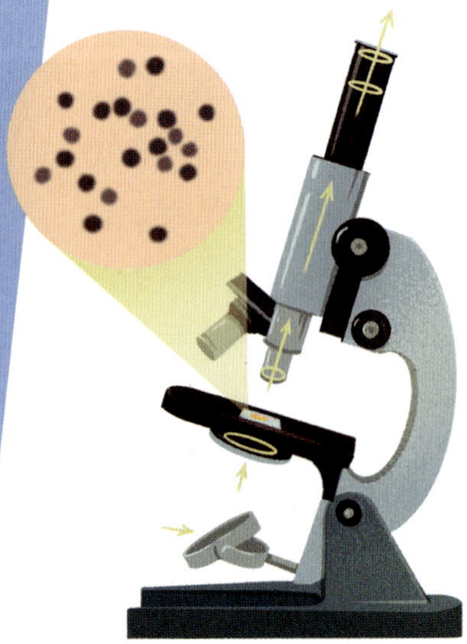

An optical microscope has glass lenses that magnify the microbes. It can help you to see microbes, like these Moraxella bacteria, found up human noses.

The image is shown on a screen.

Colors are added to the picture to make it clearer.

A scanning electron microscope or SEM is more powerful and can give you a more close-up 3D image, like these Moraxella.

NOSE: PAGE 47

How tiny?

To measure and describe the size of organisms, scientists use extra-small measurements, such as micrometers (µm) and nanometres (nm).

Millimeters (mm) are the smallest measurements on most rulers.

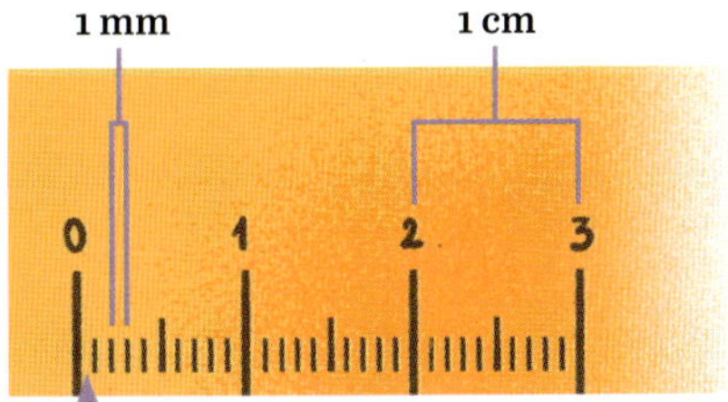

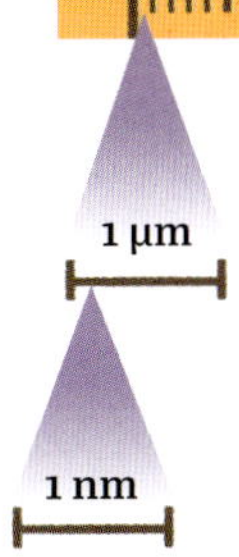

A micrometer is 1/1000th of a millimeter.

And a nanometer is 1/1000th of a micrometer (or 1 millionth of a mm)!

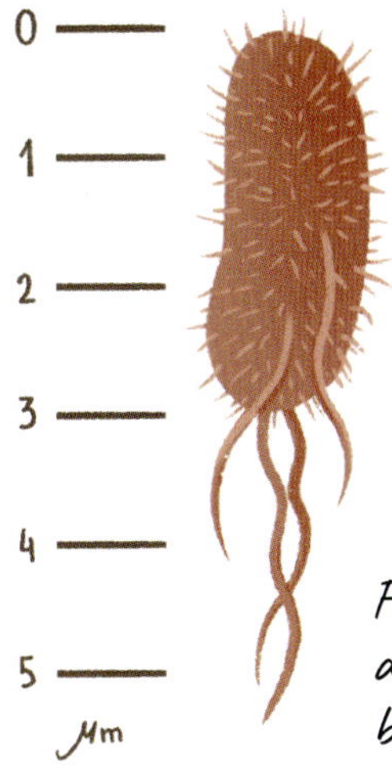

For example, a Salmonella bacterium is about 3 µm long.

BACTERIA:
PAGE 70

Microbes rule the world

Microbes have a big effect on other living things in many different ways:

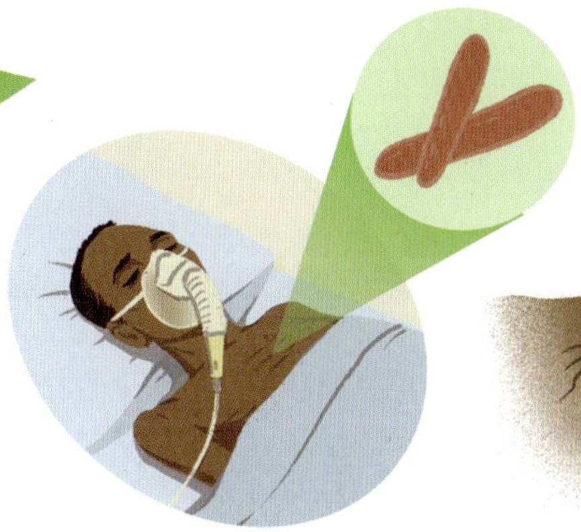

- Some are germs that can cause illnesses, such as tuberculosis or food poisoning.

- In the soil, many microorganisms help plants to grow.

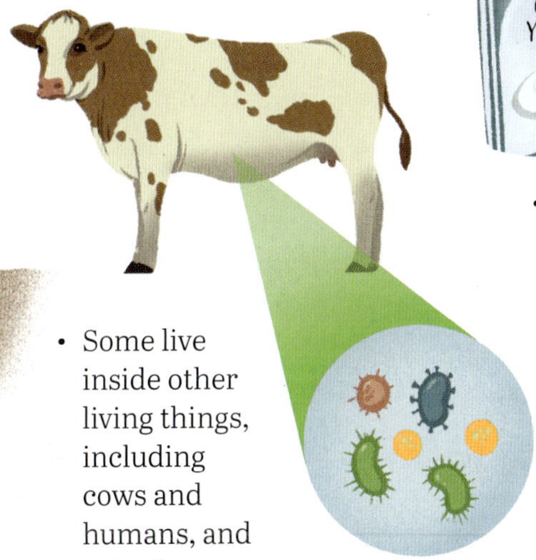

- Some live inside other living things, including cows and humans, and help them to digest food.

- Some make food go bad and decay, while others can change it to make new kinds of food, such as yogurt and soy sauce.

FOOD:
PAGE 50

Discovering microbes

For most of history, we didn't even know about microorganisms, as they are too small to see without a microscope. We had to invent microscopes first!

Antonie van Leeuwenhoek was one of the first people to see microbes, using his own homemade microscope.

BIOLOGISTS:
PAGE 8

Types of microorganisms

Scientists have discovered more than 100,000 species of microorganism, but they think there are many more still waiting to be found.

Microorganisms come in two main groups: prokaryotes and eukaryotes.

Prokaryotes include bacteria and archaea. Their cells are small and simple, with not many parts.

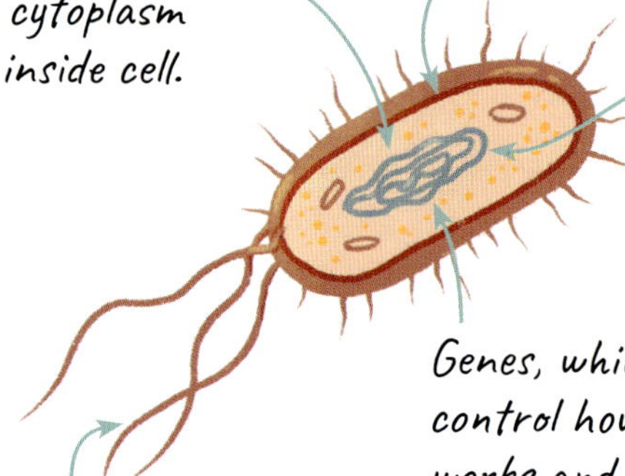

Single-celled fungi, and protists such as algae and amoebas, are eukaryotes.

Their cells are bigger, with more parts inside.

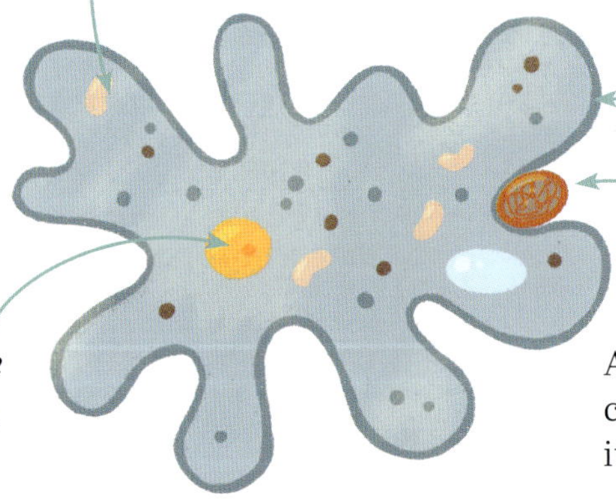

An amoeba can change shape to help it move or feed.

Though they are all very small, different microorganisms work in different ways and live in different habitats or surroundings.

Bacteria and archaea

Bacteria and archaea are two separate groups, but they look quite similar.

Bacteria are usually round or sausage-shaped. They can be harmful or helpful to other living things, and some cause diseases.

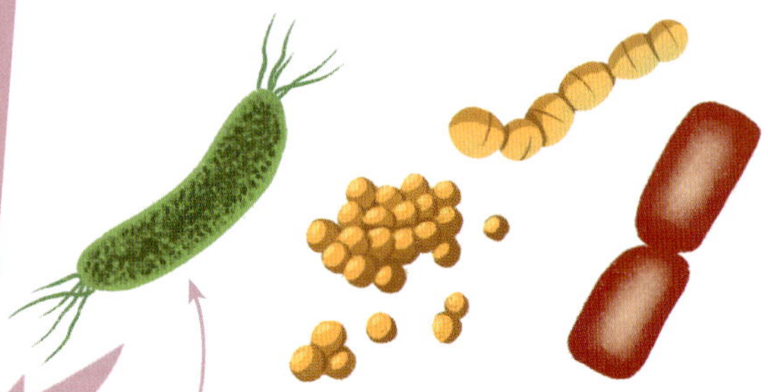

Aliivibrio fischeri is a glowing bacteria. It often lives inside sea creatures, such as glowing squid, and gives them their light.

SQUID: PAGE 25

Archaea come in a variety of shapes. They don't usually cause diseases, but often live in extreme habitats, such as very hot, dry, or salty places.

Sulfolobus archaea are thermophilic, meaning they like heat. They're often found living in hot springs.

Single-celled fungi

Singe-celled fungi, including yeasts, often live in soil or on other living things. Some are found in seawater.

Candida vini yeast lives on the skins of grapes and other fruit.

FRUIT: PAGE 59

Single-celled algae

Algae are related to plants, and like them, they use sunlight to help them make their own food. Some algae, like seaweed, have many cells, but others are single-celled microorganisms.

Chlorella is a type of single-celled algae that often grows in fish tanks, turning the water green.

FISH: PAGE 23

Other protists

Protists also include a variety of other single-celled microorganisms. They sometimes behave like tiny, single-celled animals, moving around, hunting, and eating their prey.

Didinium is a protist that lives in water and feeds on another type of protist: Paramecium.

FINDING FOOD: PAGE 28

Germs and diseases

Some microorganisms can invade or infect other living things and cause diseases. They do this because it's what they need to do to survive and reproduce.

Microorganisms that can cause diseases are known as germs. To cause an illness, a germ usually has to get onto or inside another living thing, sometimes called the "host."

Many different types of microorganisms can act as germs.

Germs can get into a host in various ways, like being breathed in, swallowed in food or water, getting into a cut or wound, or from an insect bite.

Bubonic plague, also known as the Black Death, is a disease that killed millions of people in the past. It was spread to humans in flea bites.

Rat caught the bacteria.

Flea bit rat and swallowed bacteria.

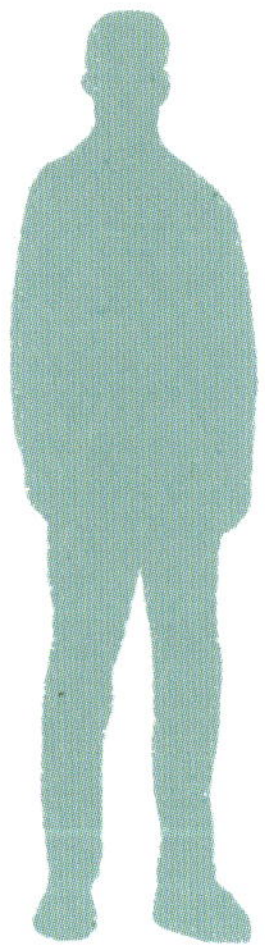

Flea bit human and spread bacteria into them.

Bacterial germs

How do bacteria make you ill? When they invade the body, they start feeding on food inside you, or even on your cells, which damages them. As they feed, they excrete—or release—toxic chemicals as waste, and these can harm your cells too.

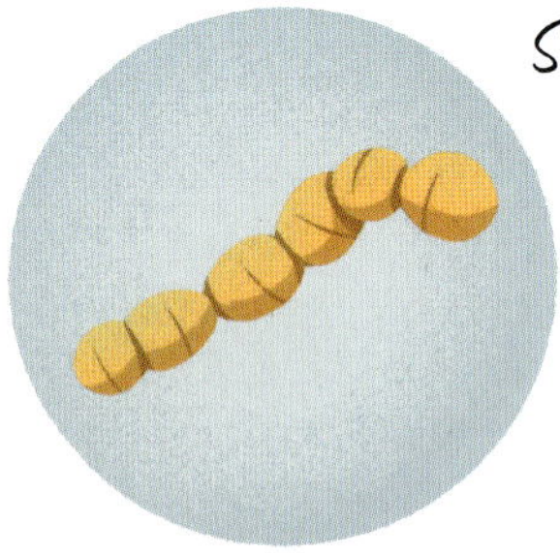

Streptococcus bacteria

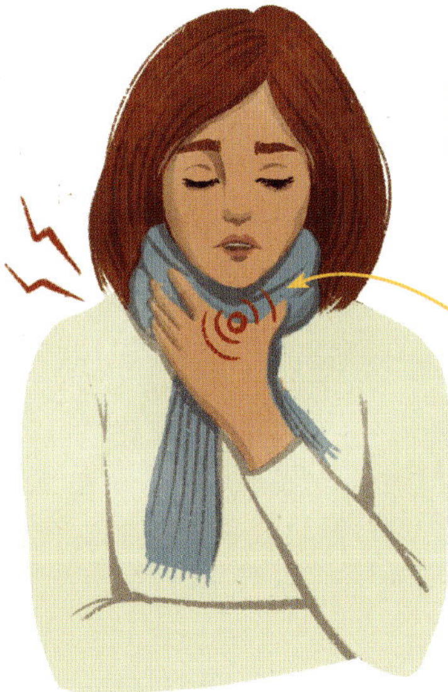

Sore throat or "strep" throat.

EXCRETION: PAGE 7

Streptococcus bacteria cause a sore throat by releasing toxins that irritate and damage the cells.

Fungal germs

Fungi often cause skin diseases, as well as diseases in plants.

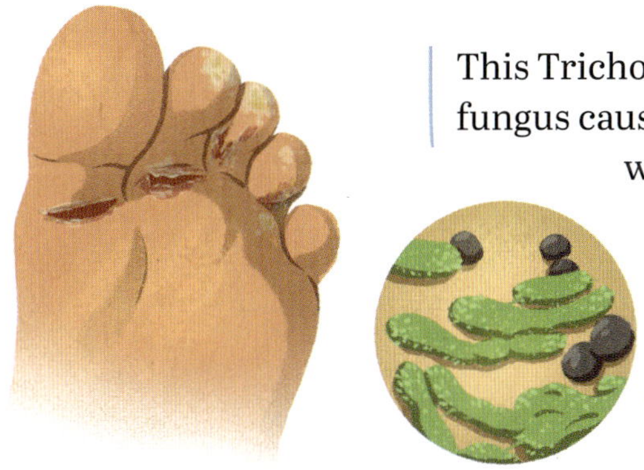

This Trichophyton single-celled fungus causes athlete's foot, which makes your toes sore and itchy.

FUNGI: PAGE 64

Protist germs

Protists are responsible for several serious illnesses, including malaria, the worst killer disease in history.

Malaria is caused by this protist, called Plasmodium.

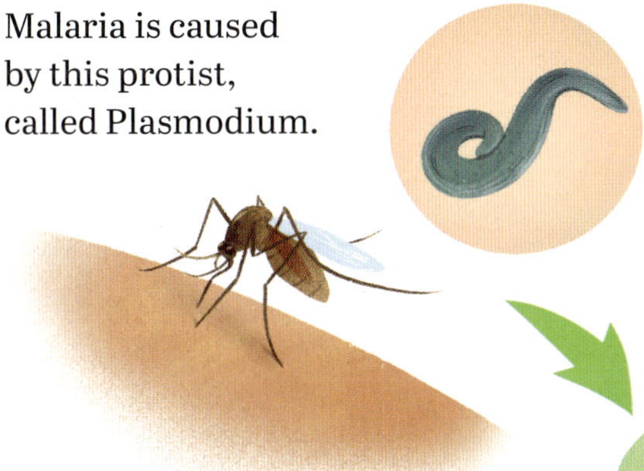

It spreads to humans in the bites of infected mosquitoes, a type of fly.

FLIES: PAGE 24

Algal germs

Even algae, another type of protist, can be germs. One type of algae can cause a disease called protothecosis in cats and dogs.

They break out of the cell and spread to other cells.

PETS: PAGE 35

Are viruses microorganisms?

Viruses are another important type of germ, causing diseases such as chickenpox, flu, Covid, and measles. However, viruses are not usually counted as microorganisms, as they are not fully alive.

This virus is attacking a cell.

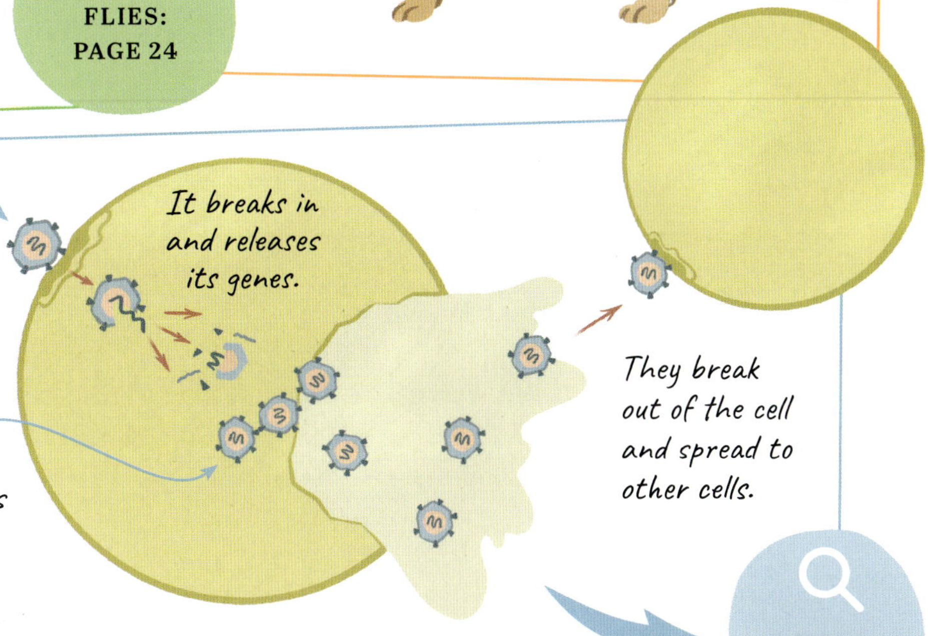

The cell is forced to use the genes to build new viruses.

They break out of the cell and spread to other cells.

Viruses reproduce by invading living cells. They take over the cell and force it to make more viruses.

CELLS: PAGE 10

Useful microorganisms

While some microorganisms can cause problems, others are useful or even essential.

Did you know that there are billions of helpful microbes living on and inside your body?

Our skin naturally has bacteria and fungi living on it. Together they're known as the skin microbiome. They keep away other, more harmful microbes, warn your body when germs land on your skin, and help to heal cuts and injuries.

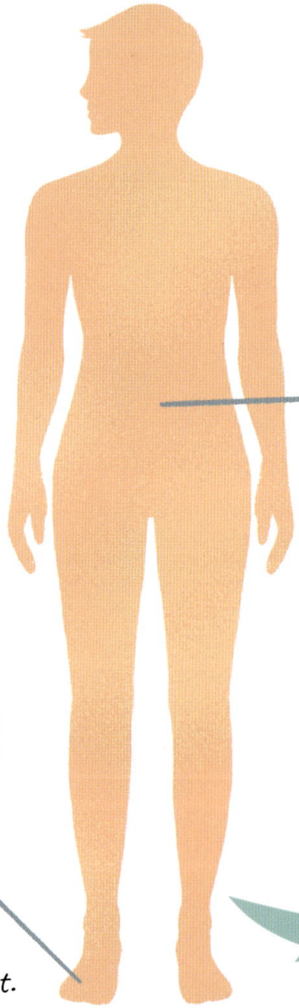

Bacteria inside the small intestine.

Inside your body, other bacteria help you to digest food and extract useful chemicals from it.

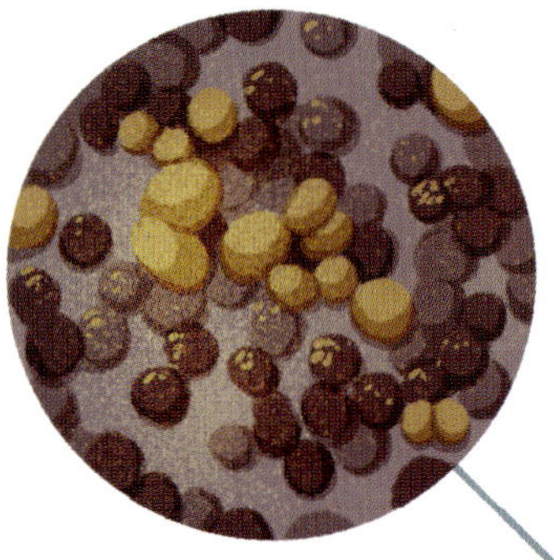

Microscope view of microbes on a human foot.

SKIN: PAGE 44

INTESTINES: PAGE 41

Helpful microorganisms also live all around us in the soil, water, and in other living things.

In the soil

Microbes are an essential part of the soil. They help plants to grow, so they are vital for helping food webs and ecosystems to keep going.

SOIL: PAGE 81

Soil microbes do several important jobs:

- Helping plant roots to soak up water and nutrients (food chemicals).
- Taking nitrogen gas, which plants need, from the atmosphere and releasing it into the soil.
- Breaking down things like dead leaves and insects into nutrients that plants can use.

A teaspoon of healthy soil contains up to a BILLION microbes, including thousands of different species.

Living together

It's not just humans that share their bodies with microbes—many other living things do too.

LIVING TOGETHER: PAGE 78

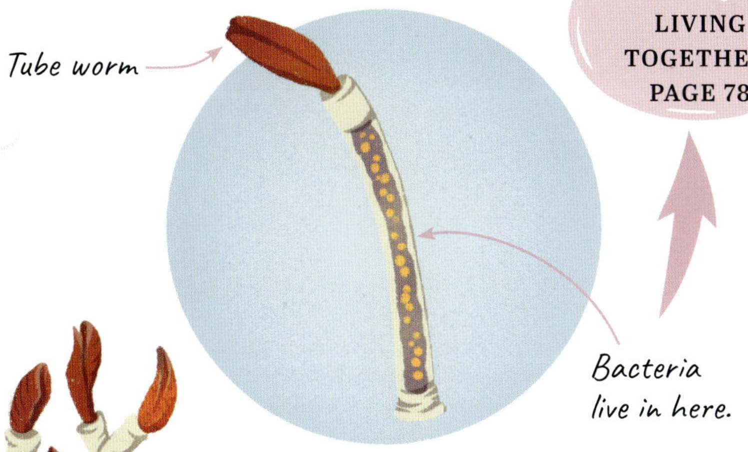

Giant tube worms live at the bottom of the sea, near hydrothermal vents, where hot water pours out from under the seabed. There's no sunlight there, so plants and algae can't use photosynthesis to make food for the ecosystem.

Instead, each tube worm has bacteria living inside it. They feed on the minerals in the hot water and make food for the tube worm. In return, the tube worm gives them a safe place to live.

Pollution eaters

Scientists have discovered microbes that can feed on some types of plastics. We could use them to clean up wild habitats and break down harmful plastic pollution into harmless substances.

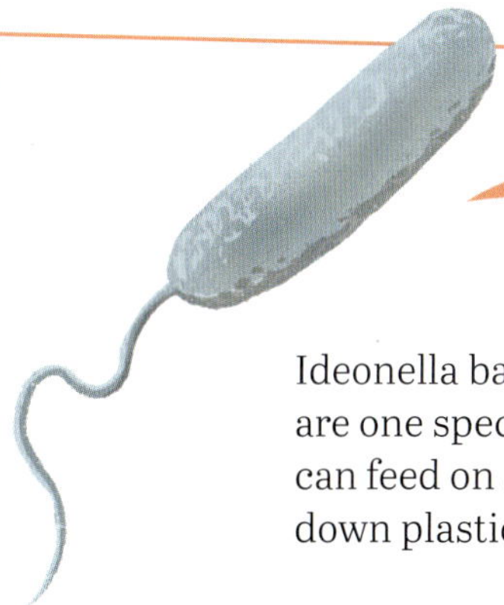

Ideonella bacteria are one species that can feed on and break down plastics.

PLASTIC POLLUTION: PAGE 83

Micro medicines

We can also use microbes against each other. Viruses work by attacking cells, and scientists have found a way to use them to treat cancer, a disease that makes some cells grow out of control.

This diagram shows how it works:

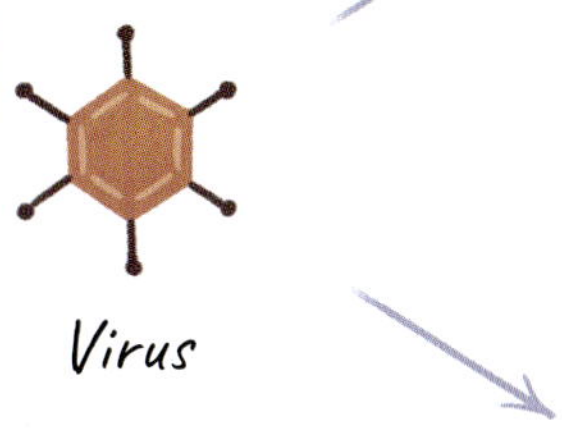

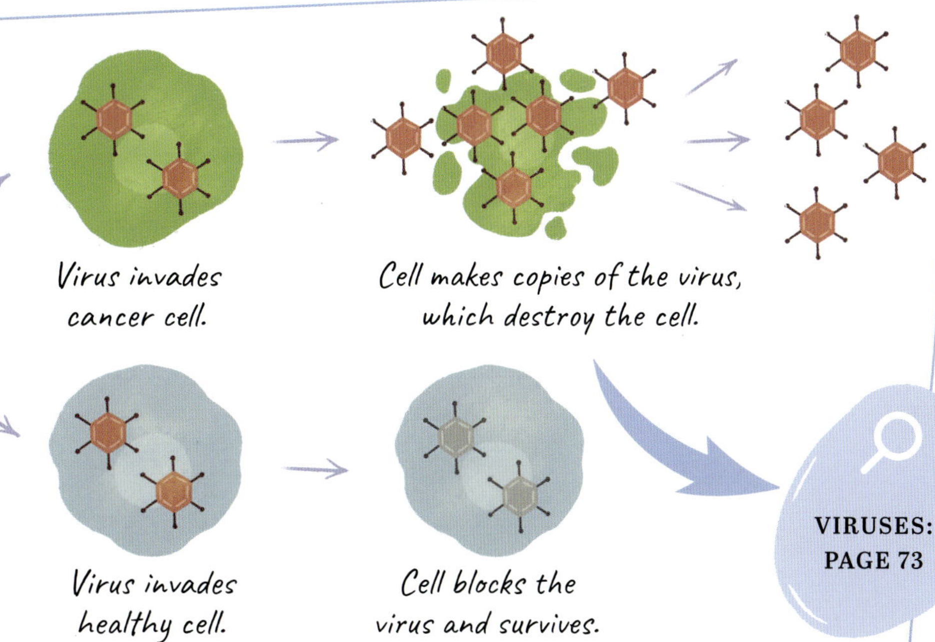

VIRUSES: PAGE 73

Habitats and biomes

A habitat is a living thing's home—the place or surroundings it lives in, such as a pond, a garden, or a deep seabed. Biomes are bigger areas with a particular type of landscape and weather, such as high mountains, or the seas and oceans.

A habitat is usually part of a larger biome.

For example, a rotting fallen tree is a habitat. It could be a home for mosses, fungi, woodlice, ants, beetles, centipedes, and millipedes.

You might find a rotting log like this in a forest, which is a type of biome.

This is a temperate forest, found in medium-warm areas.

There are many kinds of habitats and several main types of biomes. Each living thing has to be able to survive in its surroundings, so living things found in different places often have different features and abilities.

Biomes of the world

There are around ten main biome types found in different parts of the world.

TREES: PAGE 57

Types of habitats

Habitats can be large, like a whole forest or ocean, or small, like an individual pond or tree.

FLOWERS: PAGE 58

- Antarctic sea ice

- A tropical beach

- An acacia tree

- A wildflower meadow

Adaptation

Thanks to evolution, each species has adapted to survive in its particular habitat.

For example, fast-moving sea creatures have often evolved a streamlined torpedo shape, which helps them move through water, even if they belong to very different animal groups.

Mako shark—a fish.

Spinner dolphin—a mammal.

Caribbean reef squid—a mollusk.

EVOLUTION: PAGE 17

Adapting to anywhere

Many species can only survive in their specific habitats. But others are good at adapting quickly to different habitats. Rats, for example, can survive in forests, grasslands, swamps, coasts, farms, and cities. They eat a wide range of foods, which has helped them to spread all over the world.

City rats often survive on our leftover food.

ANIMAL FOOD: PAGE 28

Living together

In most habitats, many different species live side by side. Together, a habitat and its living things are known as an ecosystem.

The study of habitats and ecosystems is called ecology. Ecologists use food chains and food webs to show the relationships between the living things in an ecosystem.

Each living thing in an ecosystem depends on others for things like food and shelter.

This red crossbill's habitat is a conifer forest in North America.

It feeds on conifer seeds, and conifer trees also give it shelter and a place to nest.

However, it has to watch out for another animal in this ecosystem—the Cooper's hawk, which hunts smaller birds, such as crossbills.

Food chains

A food chain shows how one living thing feeds on another in a sequence.

Food chains usually start with plants or algae, which use photosynthesis to make food using sunlight.

This is a food chain in the Antarctic Ocean.

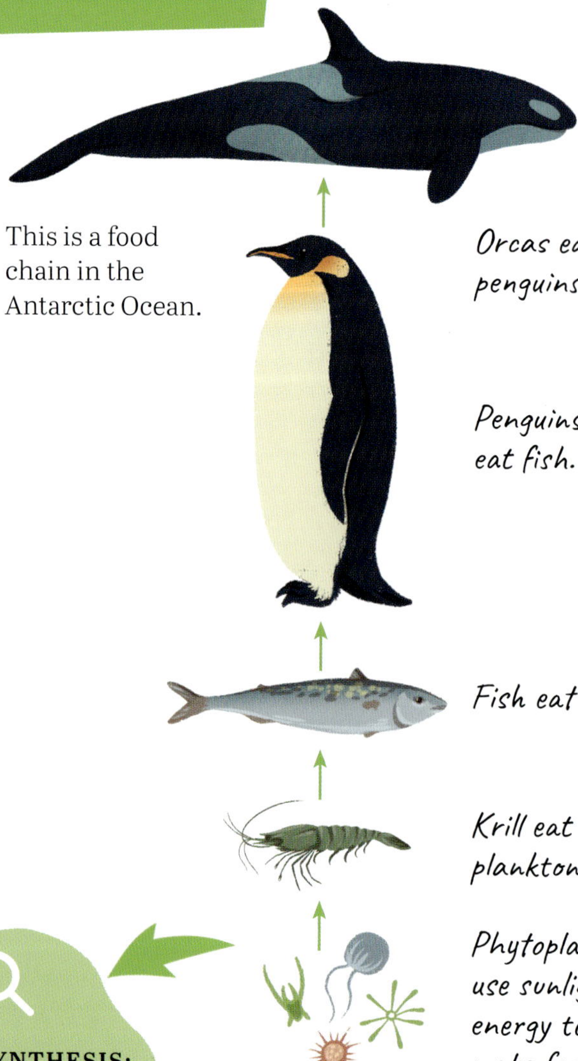

PHOTOSYNTHESIS: PAGE 54

Food webs

In most ecosystems, lots of food chains intertwine with each other to make a more complex food web.

The Antarctic Ocean food chain opposite is part of a much bigger food web, like this:

WHALES: PAGE 27

In a balance

Ecosystems exist in a delicate balance. If one species disappears, increases or decreases, it affects everything in that ecosystem.

In shallow Caribbean seas, green turtles feed on seagrass. Tiger sharks feed on the turtles.

If there are fewer sharks because of overfishing, there are too many turtles and they eat all the seagrass.

That destroys food and shelter for small sea creatures.

It also increases global warming, as seagrass plays a big part in soaking up carbon dioxide from the atmosphere.

GLOBAL WARMING: PAGE 84

Biodiversity

Biodiversity means the wide range of living things. It's important to keep as much biodiversity as possible, to help to keep ecosystems healthy.

Healthy ecosystems help to keep the air, soil, and water healthy too, so they affect all living things on Earth.

Healthy soil contains a wide range of microbes and material from dead, rotted plants, animals, and fungi—more biodiversity means healthier soil.

MICROBES: PAGE 68

Round and round

As living things become food for other things, energy gets passed on, in the form of food chemicals. It moves around in a cycle through a series of stages called "trophic levels."

The trophic levels can be shown as a pyramid diagram like this:

At each level, there are different types of living things, which pass on their energy to the next level.

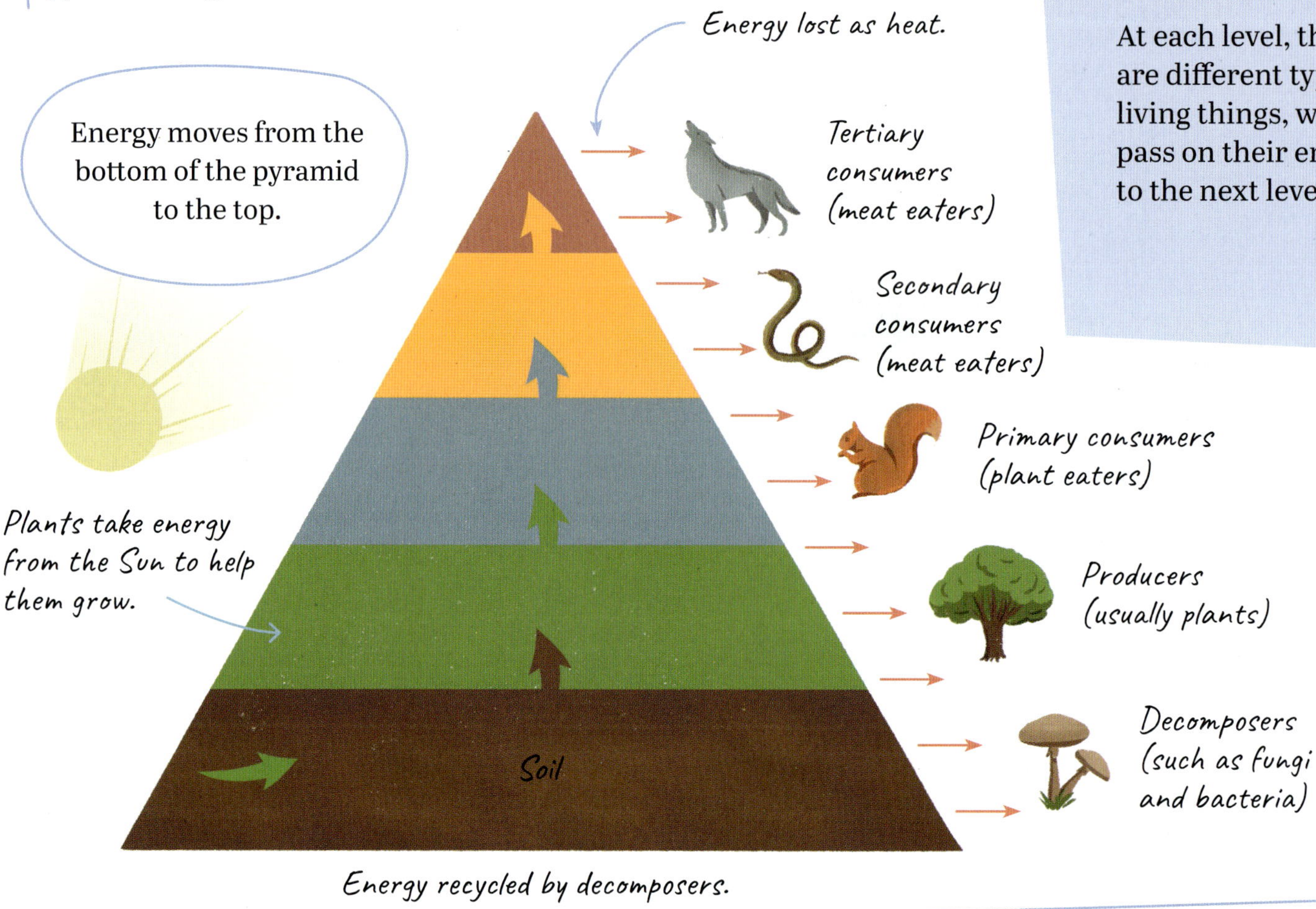

Energy recycled by decomposers.

Producers

Producers are mainly plants, or other living things that use photosynthesis.

Producers provide energy for the cycle by capturing energy from the Sun and using it to make food chemicals.

An oak tree absorbs light energy from the Sun and makes food that helps it to grow.

TREES: PAGE 57

Primary consumers

Primary consumers are plant-eaters, or herbivores.

When plant-eaters eat plants, the energy in the plants is passed on into their bodies, helping them to grow.

A squirrel gets energy by eating the oak tree's acorns.

MAMMALS: PAGE 23

Secondary and tertiary consumers

Secondary and tertiary consumers are meat-eaters, or carnivores.

HUNTING: PAGE 29

A hunter at the top of the pyramid, such as a wolf, is called an apex predator.

Secondary consumers hunt plant-eaters, and tertiary consumers hunt other meat-eaters.

For example, a snake might eat a squirrel ...

.... and a wolf might then eat the snake.

Decomposers

Not all of the energy passes up to the next level. Some escapes as heat, and in poop and other waste. And some living things die without being eaten.

Waste such as poop and the bodies of dead living things contain energy too. They are fed on by decomposers, such as fungi, bacteria, and earthworms.

As they feed, decomposers break the waste down into chemicals in the soil. They help plants to grow, starting the cycle again.

FUNGI: PAGE 64

Human impacts

Humans first evolved around 2 million years ago, and since then we have made big changes to the planet—especially in the last few hundred years. This has had a huge impact on the world's other living things.

Some of the changes we've made include:

- Cutting down at least one third of the world's forests, to make space for cities, farms, and roads.

- Hunting some wild animal species until they died out.

- Releasing large amounts of pollution, such as vehicle exhaust, factory waste, and litter, which can damage natural habitats and harm wildlife.

Human activities can cause problems for nature and wildlife in a variety of ways. They can sometimes cause problems for us too.

Habitat loss

A living thing's habitat is its natural home or surroundings. For example, spider monkeys live in tropical forests, and frogs live in ponds or swamps.

Many species cannot survive without their natural habitats. So if a forest is cut down or a swamp is filled in to build houses on, some species have nowhere to live and could die out.

Asian elephants have lost over 60 percent of their natural forest habitat, and what is left is broken up by roads, railways, and farms, making it harder for them to move around.

HABITATS: PAGE 76

Hunting and fishing

Humans have always hunted wild animals and caught fish from seas and rivers—mainly for food, but also for things like fur, feathers, and ivory (made from elephant tusks).

ENDANGERED SPECIES: PAGE 86

If we hunt or fish too many of a species, its population falls and it can become endangered or die out.

The scalloped hammerhead shark is endangered because of overfishing. It is caught mainly for its fins, which are used to make a kind of soup.

Using things up

Another problem is that there are so many humans: over 8 billion. So we use a LOT of food, water, space, and materials.

For example, crops like avocados, sugar, and alfalfa need a lot of water. If farmers use water from rivers for their crops, the rivers can dry up.

When a river runs dry, animals and plants lose their habitats and water source. It can be bad for local communities too, as they lose their water supply.

CROPS: PAGE 62

Pollution problems

Pollution is one of the worst problems caused by humans.

GLOBAL WARMING: PAGE 84

There are many types of pollution with a variety of effects.

- Chemicals from mines and factories can poison rivers and seawater.
- Plastic litter clogs waterways and can harm sea creatures that eat it.
- Smoke and gases from vehicles and power stations are harmful to breathe in.
- Weed killers and pesticides used on farms harm or kill wildlife.
- Some waste gases from burning fuel trap heat in the atmosphere, making the Earth warm up.

Climate changes

The Earth is gradually getting warmer, a phenomenon known as global warming. This changes the climate, or weather patterns, and affects natural habitats and living things.

Climate change is happening all over the world, and is affecting living things, including humans, in a wide range of ways.

The Earth's temperature and climate have always changed naturally over time. But the climate change that is happening now is unusually fast, and has been caused by humans.

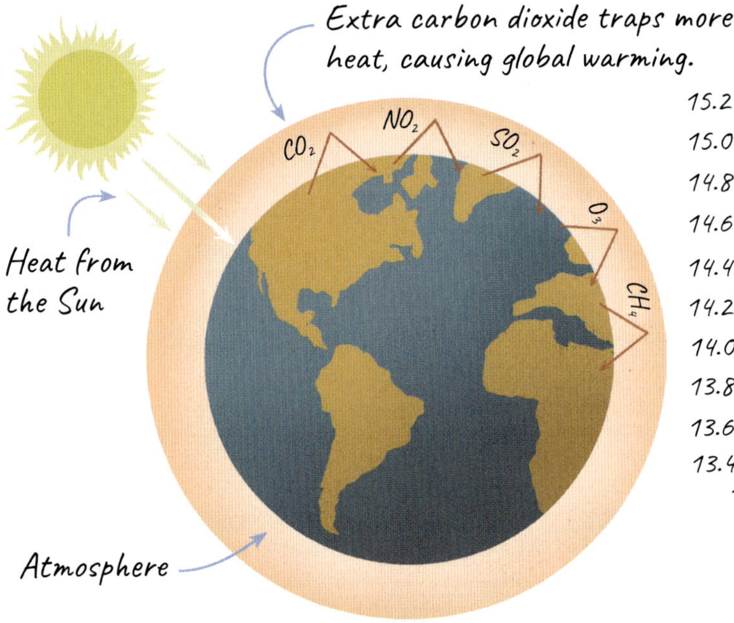

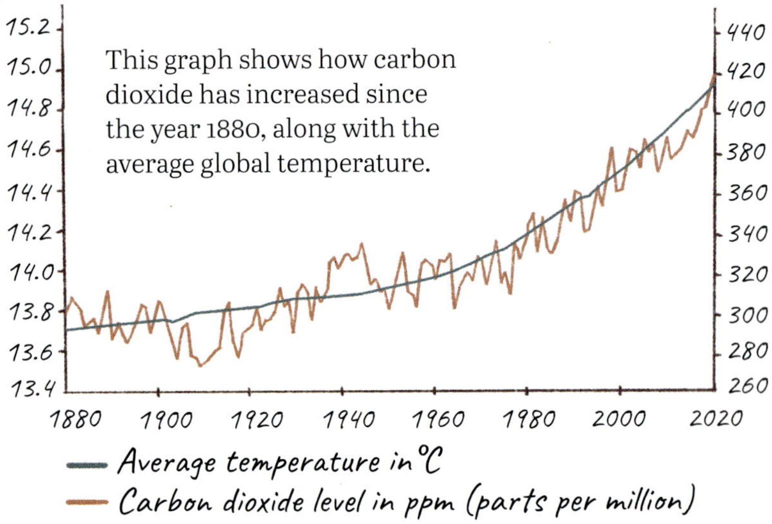

This graph shows how carbon dioxide has increased since the year 1880, along with the average global temperature.

The world is warming because of a process called the greenhouse effect. Gases in the atmosphere, including carbon dioxide, trap heat from the Sun. This is normal, and helps to keep the world warm enough for living things. But humans burn a huge amount of fuel in factories, power stations, and vehicles, and this releases extra carbon dioxide.

Heating up

Higher temperatures can cause ...

- Heatwaves: periods of very hot, dry weather.

Plants and animals can overheat or run out of water.

- Heatwaves can lead to dangerous wildfires.

Wildfires kill animals and destroy forests.

- Desertification: dry areas get drier and become deserts.

Plants die, affecting ecosystems and food chains.

FOOD CHAINS: PAGE 78

Weird weather

The extra heat energy can cause ...

- More powerful storms, especially hurricanes and cyclones.

Strong winds blow down trees.

TREES: PAGE 57

- More water evaporating from the sea, causing heavier rain and more floods.

Floods are dangerous for burrowing animals.

Acid oceans

Some of the extra carbon dioxide in the air gets dissolved in sea water, making the water more acidic.

The acidic water damages and weakens the shells of sea creatures like snails, mussels, and clams.

Pteropods are tiny sea mollusks, some with clear shells, which are being damaged by acidic seawater.

Habitat loss

As well as being dangerous for living things, the effects of climate change are also destroying habitats, which can make it much harder for some species to survive.

HABITATS: PAGE 76

Although they can swim, polar bears need sea ice to hunt and rest on.

- Wildfires destroy forests and grasslands.
- Rising sea levels could completely cover some low-lying island habitats.
- Warmer, more acidic oceans can kill coral reefs, a habitat for many species.
- Sea ice is melting, making it harder for polar bears to hunt seals.

Endangered and extinct

An endangered species is a living thing that's at risk of dying out and no longer existing. When that happens, it's called going extinct.

Species have always died out, since life first began. That's why there are so many prehistoric species that are no longer around. But thanks to human activities, a lot of today's species are in danger.

The mountain gorilla is an endangered species.

Its population has fallen because of habitat loss, hunting, and wars in the areas where it lives.

The St. Helena olive tree became extinct in 2003.

It died out because of habitat loss and being eaten by farm animals.

Biologists and ecologists work hard to keep track of the numbers of different species, so that they can find out which are the most endangered.

Keeping count

Scientists use several methods to keep track of how many of a species there are.

- Spotting and counting plants, animals, or fungi on foot.
- Flying over landscapes and taking photos to study afterward.
- Looking for signs left by animals, such as footprints and droppings.
- Using camera traps that take a photo when an animal passes by.
- Collecting information from the public—for example, in garden bird surveys.
- Recording sounds, such as birdsong and whale calls.

A pygmy hippo caught on camera.

This biologist is setting up a camera trap in a forest habitat to take photos of pygmy hippos at night.

CONSERVATION: PAGE 88

Making changes

The conservation status of a species can change over time. Sometimes, a species can recover and become less endangered.

Giant pandas used to be EN (Endangered), but breeding programs have increased their population. In 2016 they were reclassified as VU (Vulnerable), meaning they are now less seriously endangered.

BREEDING: PAGE 89

Conservation status

An organization called the IUCN (International Union for Conservation of Nature) collects the data on each species and gives it a "Conservation status," or category. The categories are:

- **EX** *Extinct*
- **EW** *Extinct in the Wild* (but some could still be alive in zoos or botanic gardens)

THREATENED:

- **CR** *Critically Endangered* (very seriously endangered)
- **EN** *Endangered*
- **VU** *Vulnerable*

- **NT** *Near Threatened*
- **LC** *Least Concern* (meaning not endangered)

CONSERVATION: PAGE 88

Endangered species education

Learning about endangered species makes it easier to protect them.

For example, people are less likely to buy things made of ivory if they know it comes from endangered elephants.

Ivory items like bangles used to be common, but are now unpopular because they harm wildlife.

HUMAN IMPACTS: PAGE 82

Conservation

Humans have caused a lot of problems for other species, but we are now trying to undo some of the damage and help endangered species to survive.

Trying to help the natural world and save other species is called conservation. Many governments around the world now include conservation in their policies, and countries also work on it together.

Conservation takes many forms, which often work together to protect wild habitats and species.

Costa Rica, a small tropical country in Central America, is a world leader in conservation.

Wildlife wardens in Costa Rica guard endangered species, such as parrots, monkeys, jaguars, and sea turtles, from hunters and egg collectors.

Wildlife reserves

A wildlife reserve, nature reserve, or national park is an area of land or sea that's set aside for wildlife. Hunting, cutting down trees, and building homes are banned, and the habitat is kept as natural and wild as possible. It is guarded by park wardens.

Wildlife guide

Wildlife reserves often use "ecotourism" to make the money they need. They charge visitors to enter the reserve and go on guided wildlife-watching tours.

HABITATS: PAGE 76

Breeding and planting

We can also help endangered animals to breed and have babies, and help plants by replanting them. This can be quicker than waiting for them to breed or spread naturally.

Seagrass is an important food and habitat in the seas and oceans, but it's often damaged by fishing and tourism. Replanting helps return seagrass to its natural habitat.

A volunteer diver replanting seagrass.

FISHING: PAGE 83

Conservation laws

Governments around the world have made national and international laws to protect wildlife, too.

There are laws against:

- Hunting or collecting endangered species
- Trading or selling endangered species or their body parts
- Polluting natural habitats
- Collecting wild animals' eggs
- Starting fires in the wild

Pangolins are mammals that are hunted for their scales, which are used to make traditional medicines. Hunting them and selling their scales has been banned in many countries.

MAMMALS: PAGE 23

Rewilding

Rewilding means returning as much land as possible to a more natural, wild state to give living things their habitats back. It includes replanting forests, and letting road verges and parts of parks and gardens grow wild.

Letting land return to its wild state means more wildflowers and weeds grow. They provide more food for insects and snails, which provide food for other wildlife, supporting a whole food web.

FOOD WEBS: PAGE 79

The variety of life

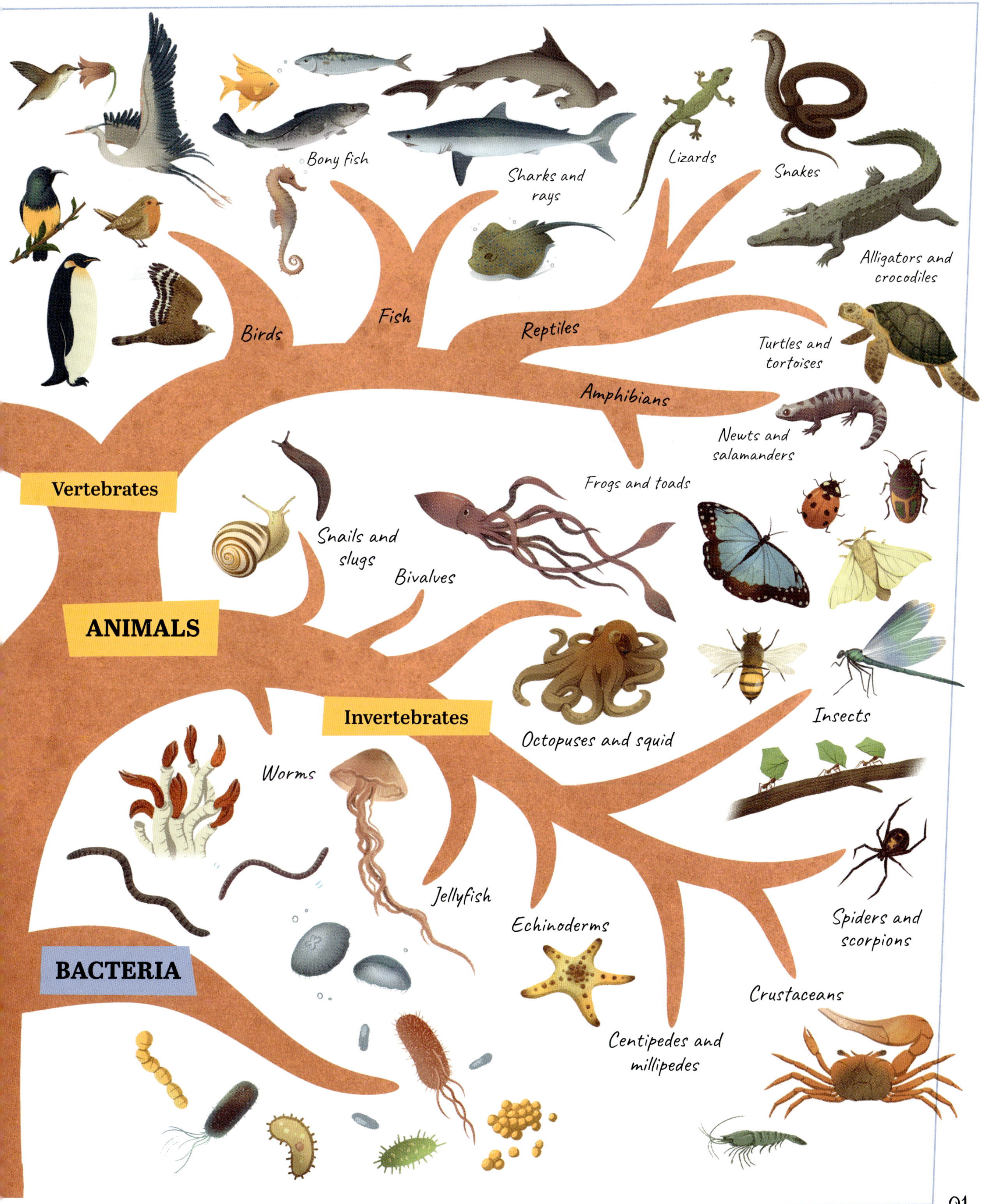
Bony fish
Sharks and rays
Lizards
Snakes
Alligators and crocodiles
Birds
Fish
Reptiles
Turtles and tortoises
Amphibians
Newts and salamanders
Frogs and toads
Vertebrates
Snails and slugs
Bivalves
ANIMALS
Octopuses and squid
Insects
Invertebrates
Worms
Jellyfish
Echinoderms
Spiders and scorpions
Crustaceans
BACTERIA
Centipedes and millipedes

Glossary

Adaptation Changing over time to suit new or changed surroundings or conditions.

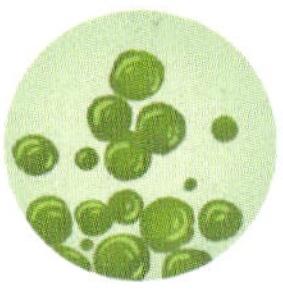

Algae A type of living thing that makes food using sunlight, similar to plants.

Amoeba A type of single-celled living thing that can move around and eat food.

Amphibian A type of vertebrate that lays eggs in water, such as frogs and newts, then later lives on land.

Antennae Sensing organs, also called feelers, that insects and some other animals have on their heads.

Antibiotics Medicines that kill bacteria.

Arteries Blood vessels that carry blood from the heart to other parts of the body.

Arthropod A type of invertebrate animal with jointed legs, such as insects, spiders, and crabs.

Bacteria Very small, single-celled microorganisms, which can sometimes act as germs.

Biodiversity The variety of living things in a particular habitat, or in the whole world..

Bird A type of vertebrate animal that has feathers and wings, and lays eggs.

Blood vessels The tubes blood flows along to travel around your body.

Camouflage Body shape, hue, or pattern that helps a living thing to hide by matching its surroundings.

Carbon dioxide (CO^2) A gas found in the air, produced as waste by animals when they breathe, and used by plants to make food.

Cartilage Tough rubbery tissue that makes up some parts of the skeleton.

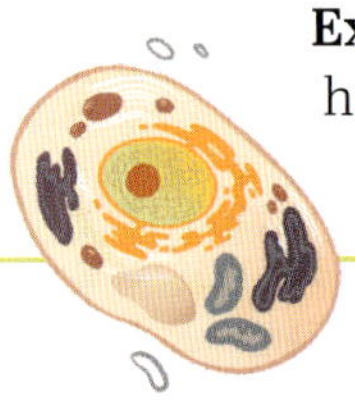

Cells The tiny units that living things are made up of.

Chlorophyll A green chemical inside plants, which they use to capture sunlight for use in photosynthesis.

Classification The process of sorting living things into a system of types and groups.

Climate The typical weather patterns in a particular place, or the world as a whole.

Climate change A long-term change in climate patterns.

Conservation Efforts to protect and preserve living species and natural habitats.

Crustacean A type of invertebrate animal that usually has a shell and many legs, such as crabs, shrimps, and woodlice.

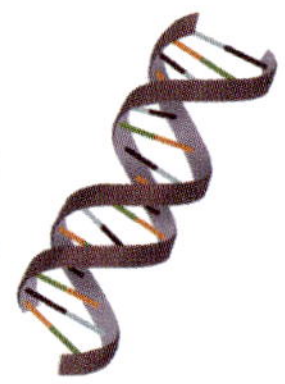

DNA (short for **DeoxyriboNucleic Acid**) A chemical found in cells, containing coded instructions that make the cell work.

Echinoderm A group of invertebrate animals with five body sections, such as starfish and sea urchins.

Ecology The study of ecosystems and how living things interact with each other.

Ecosystem A habitat and the variety of living things that live in it.

Ecotourism Going to visit wild areas and watching wildlife as a vacation, holiday, or day out.

Endangered At risk of dying out and becoming extinct.

Eukaryote A living thing with cells that contain a nucleus and organelles.

Evolution A process of gradual change over multiple generations of living things.

Exoskeleton A hard outer shell or skin found in many invertebrates, such as beetles.

Extinct An extinct species is one that has died out and no longer exists.

Field "In the field" means in the wild, or in a living thing's natural habitat.

Fish A type of vertebrate water animal with a skeleton, fins, and gills.

Food chain A sequence of living things in which each feeds on the one before.

Food web A network of plants and animals in an ecosystem that depend on each other for food.

Fossil The remains, or traces, of a prehistoric living thing, preserved in rock.

Fungi A group of living things that are not plants or animals. They include mushrooms, molds, and yeast.

Genes Sequences of chemicals arranged along strands of DNA, which act as coded instructions for cells.

Germs Tiny living things that can cause diseases in other living things.

Gills Breathing organs found in fish and some amphibians, which allow them to extract oxygen from water.

Global warming A gradual increase in Earth's average temperature over the last two centuries, caused by human activities.

Habitat The natural home or surroundings of a living thing.

Habitat loss The destruction of wild natural habitats.

Host A living thing that is used as a home or food source by a parasite or germ.

Instinct A built-in, automatic pattern of activity in a living thing.

Intestines Tubes inside the body that extract useful chemicals from food and collect waste.

Invertebrate An animal that does not have a backbone (or any bones at all).

Ivory A material made from elephant tusks or other animal teeth.

Joints The parts of a skeleton where bones join together.

Lab Short for laboratory, a room or building where scientists do tests or experiments.

Larva A baby animal that has a different form than its parents, such as a caterpillar.

Life cycle The series of changes a living thing goes through as it is born, grows, becomes an adult, and reproduces, or has babies.

Mammal A group of animals, such as cows, dogs, and humans, that feed their babies on milk.

Marsupial A group of mammals that carry their babies in a pouch on the mother's underside, such as kangaroos and koalas.

Microbiology The study of microscopic living things.

Microorganism A living creature that is too small for us to see with the naked eye.

Mollusk A group of soft-bodied invertebrates, such as snails and octopuses.

Monitoring Keeping track of a wild species and checking on its numbers, health, or movements.

Mold A type of fungus that often grows on old food or in damp places.

Mycelium A network of threads that grows into and over a food supply.

Nectar A sugary liquid made inside flowers to attract insects and other animals to pollinate a plant.

Nitrogen An element found in the air as a gas, and also as an important part of soil and living things.

Nucleus A part inside some cells that contains DNA and controls how the cell works.

Nutrient Any substance that a living thing needs for energy or growth.

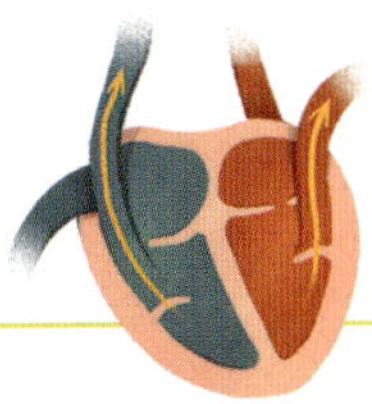

Organ A body part that does a particular job, like the brain, heart, or stomach.

Organelle Part of a cell that does a particular job.

Oxygen A gas found in the air that animals breathe in and plants release as a waste gas.

Parasite A living thing that lives in or on another living thing and uses it for food.

Pesticide A chemical used to kill pests, such as insects that eat crops.

Phloem Tubes inside plants that carry food around the plant.

Photosynthesis The process of using energy from the Sun to convert water and carbon dioxide gas into food, which happens inside a plant's leaves.

Plankton Tiny living things that drift around in sea or pond water.

Plasma The liquid part of blood, which carries blood cells along in it.

Pollen Tiny yellow grains released by male flowers or parts of flowers that help female flowers, or parts of flowers, to make seeds.

Pollinate To carry or spread pollen from one flower to another.

Pollinator An animal that pollinates plants, such as a honeybee or a hummingbird.

Predator An animal that hunts and eats other animals.

Prehistoric From the time before history was first written down, around 5,000 years ago.

Prey An animal that is hunted and eaten by another animal.

Primates A group of mammals with flexible hands and feet and good eyesight, including monkeys, chimpanzees, and humans.

Prokaryotes Single-celled living things with no nucleus in their cells, such as bacteria and archaea.

Protists A group of living things that include algae and amoebas.

Reproduce To have babies, or make more living things of the same species.

Reptiles A group of vertebrates that usually have scales and lay eggs, including lizards and crocodiles.

Selective breeding Choosing the most useful plants and animals to breed as farm animals and crops.

Species The scientific name for a particular type of living thing.

Spinal cord A bundle of nerves that runs down the middle of the back, found only in vertebrate animals.

Spores Tiny seed-like parts that fungi and some plants and bacteria release to reproduce.

Stomata Tiny holes on the surface of leaves that let gases in and out.

Toxin A substance that is poisonous to cells or a particular species.

Veins Blood vessels that carry blood from different parts of the body to the heart.

Vertebrae The spinal bones, or backbone, down the middle of the back.

Vertebrate An animal with a backbone.

Virus A type of tiny germ, much smaller than most bacteria, that reproduces by invading the cells of living things.

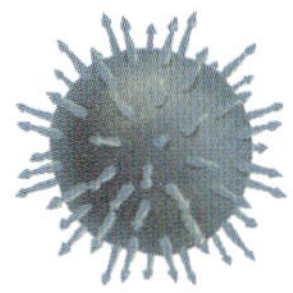

Wildlife reserve A wild area set aside for wildlife and protected to stop it from being changed or damaged by humans.

Xylem Tubes inside plants that carry water around the plant.

Yeast A type of single-celled fungus.

Index

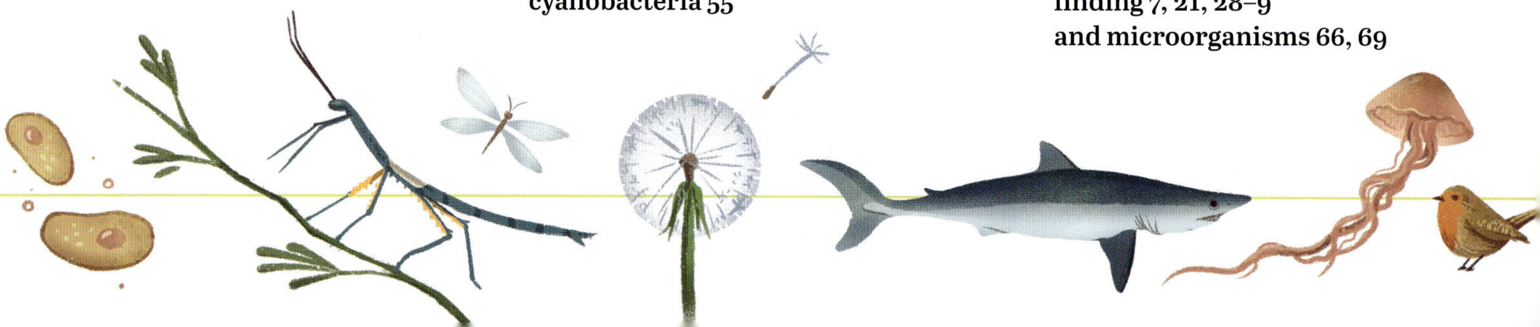